THE DIET WATCHERS GOURMET COOKBOOK

by Ann Gold and Sara Welles Briller

Published in Association with *Parade Magazine*

GROSSET & DUNLAP
Publishers / New York
A NATIONAL GENERAL COMPANY

With deep gratitude to my husband, Al Gold, my daughters Michelle and Sharyn, and to Seth Richard and Robert D. Weissman for all their help in allowing me to create and work with Diet Watchers. Also, my thanks to my lecturers for their dedication to the people who come to Diet Watchers.

—ANN GOLD

. . . And my thanks to Bert Briller, to Joan and Robbie, and to Louise Siler for their continued encouragement and patience through the time I needed to help create this new book.

—SARA WELLES BRILLER

CONTENTS

About Ann Gold   7

About Sara Welles Briller   10

Make a Plan   15

What You Should Know   16

You Have To Have a System   20

My System Today   21

How I Cook Today   22

Other Systems   22

The Secret of DW One Pot Cooking   22

Do You Have the Energy?   23

Why Fuss?   24

Life Can Be Simpler   25

Around the World Gourmet Recipes   26

    The Italian Hand   27

    French Delicacies   39

    A Touch of Jewish   52

    Side Trips   62

    Skol in Scandinavia   77

Russian Holiday 81

Middle Eastern Intrigue 85

Exotics of the Far East 93

North of the Border 109

Some Latin Pleasures 112

As American As . . . 115

Guessing Games 128

Parties Are For Slimming 130

Menu Plans 141

Never on Sunday 154

Work Sheets 155

So Be A Cook! 158

THE DIET WATCHERS GOURMET COOKBOOK

ABOUT ANN GOLD

Ann Gold has helped thousands of people to lose fat—and to enjoy good health—since 1963 when she founded Diet Watchers.

A chic brunette who enjoys a size nine figure, Ann Gold knows what it means to be fat. She was a 13 pound baby at birth, she weighed 65 pounds by the time she was two years old, was 155 pounds all through her teens and for most of her adult life (she is a wife, mother and grandmother) she was an obese 185 pounds.

She tried to trim down many times—this diet, that fad, the "fat doctors"—you name it. Nothing worked well enough or for very long, until in 1961 she went on the diet developed by the late Dr. Norman Joliffe which was then being used by the New York City Board of Health to help obese patients lose weight. This was based on a nutritious eating plan that eliminated most fats and sugars and worked to change body chemistry.

In twenty weeks she took off 65 pounds. Even more exciting, as every dieter will appreciate, she knew she had finally found a way to maintain her new, lithe, youthful figure. She has remained slim, kept her 120 pound figure, ever since 1961. And having found the way finally to fight back at a world that once taunted her as "Fatso!" she now gets lasting satisfaction from sharing her hard won diet watching secrets with others.

When she first went on the diet, Ann Gold was a highly successful saleswoman of mutual funds. But slimness was so important to her that she decided to get her overweight husband and her two overweight daughters to reduce. Working with them, she discovered how different people react differently to foods. She began experimenting with

7

eating patterns to learn the individual timing, selections and food combinations that could help each person in her own family to lose fat most quickly.

After her own husband and daughters had gotten their weights down to desirable goals she tackled the tough problem (as every fat person knows) of *maintaining* slim figures. She concentrated on the techniques that work for each individual. She found many successful patterns and, equally, important, how to teach them.

A physician impressed with her practical results and sensible approach and who knew how many patients desperately need to lose weight suggested in 1963 that she form classes to help them. So she started the first Diet Watchers group. These group members who lost weight were asked by friends, "How did you do it?" And their friends began to come. Ann soon found herself conducting group sessions seven days a week, until there were successful graduates whom she began to teach to step in and lead groups using her techniques.

Doctors have been among Diet Watchers' biggest boosters. They have sent patients with heart trouble, diabetes and other problems aggravated by obesity.

By 1968, when the first Diet Watchers Guide—a basic handbook—appeared, there were 23 groups along the Eastern seaboard. By 1969 there were 80 groups in the U.S., some as far west as Arizona and Texas—and European and Australian groups were in the offing.

By 1961 she was beginning to franchise nationally and internationally, forming groups that used her techniques in every state and in other countries of the world

From the beginning, Ann Gold could use a special skill as a cook, as a weapon in her fight against fat. She had grown up in the kitchen of her father's successful food catering business in New York City, and she adapted her knowledge about good eating to the needs of diet watching. Today for the people in her groups, who come from many ethnic and national backgrounds she also constantly creates new interesting exotic foods. All her cooking skill has been wedded to the Diet Watchers program, for she uses only foods and techniques that enable you to lose fat, while you eat well.

Ann Gold makes no medical claims. She is not a doctor, not a nutritionist, not a psychologist, although she majored in psychology at college. But her techniques work. They have been proven practical and effective by thousands and thousands of people in Diet Watchers groups.

The recipes in this book have not appeared between covers before. They have appeared on tables and earned compliments from Diet Watchers and international gourmets.

For further information about
Diet Watchers Franchises, write to—
DIET WATCHERS FRANCHISES, LTD
31 Lenore Avenue
Monsey, New York 10952

ABOUT
SARA WELLES BRILLER

An author, editor and journalist, and a former columnist, Sara Welles Briller has made her life career in communications.

The challenge of translating the support and special techniques of diet group meetings into book form was first levelled at her in 1966 when two friends, one of whom had suffered a heart attack, lost many unhealthy pounds at Diet Watchers meetings in White Plains, New York, and insisted that she go down to see and report what was happening. The result was the Diet Watchers Guide, which immediately became a national best seller.

Sara Welles was never a "fatty." Instead she was a "skinny" active child and adolescent who remembers how parents and teachers worried over her "small" appetite. But as an adult she found herself, like many, caught between too many ample business lunches and too many deadline pressured sandwich-at-the-desk meals. This kind of eating became an occupational hazard for her, as they are for most of us. She began to worry about her diet, counted calories, took pounds off and put them on again. While writing the Diet Watchers Guide she went on the diet herself as a test and quickly dropped eight pounds that had been especially stubborn about leaving. She has kept them off easily since.

At present Sara Welles is Project Editor for a New York book publisher. She has collaborated on several books, including "Born Female: The High Cost of Keeping Women Down." She was one of the first staff members of Parade Magazine, today the country's most successful Sunday newspaper supplement, and for a number of years, as Senior Editor, wrote a widely quoted column, "A Woman's

View," for Printers Ink Magazine. She has also been Articles Editor of the Woman's Home Companion, a senior editor of House & Garden, and an editor for Mademoiselle, Charm and Living for Young Homemakers. Her articles have appeared in Family Circle, Seventeen and many other national magazines. She is a member of the Society of Magazine Writers.

To this *The Diet Watchers Gourmet Cookbook* she also brings her own interest in world cuisines, which comes from her travels, from work with many cookbooks and her familiarity with New York's celebrated international restaurants.

She lives in Larchmont, New York with her husband Bert Briller, a television executive, and their two teenagers, Joan and Robert.

INTRODUCTION

When the Diet Watchers Guide—our basic manual—first appeared in 1968 it became an immediate best seller. It also began an avalanche of letters from women and men to the authors telling us how much the Guide had done for them. People wanted copies for themselves, to send to friends and relatives—even in other countries—or to join groups, or permission to start new "franchise" groups.

The hunger of people to learn more of the new healthful cooking was also clear.

Now, cooking techniques are vital for Diet Watchers. We had published about 125 basic recipes in our basic Guide, in order to help readers begin their programs. But anyone who wants to get slim and keep slim must do more than make a beginning.

People start diets every day. The trick is to stay on it as long as you need to, until you reach your true goal.

For it you need something more—something like a whole new cuisine. You need, in short, adequate *variety* to remain interested in the foods you will eat.

No one using any book—cooking or dieting or entertainment book with recipes—uses every recipe in it. You choose from what is there. You try only a few recipes, learn them, stick with them and use them over and over and finally, inevitably, you tire of them.

This is the danger point. Because right now, bit by bit, you'll begin to slide back into your old cooking and eating habits. Not because you want the old *foods*. Because you are looking for something—you don't know what. *You are*

12

just looking for something different. What you must do now if you would stop yourself from sinking back into the old fattening cooking is to broaden your knowledge of the new way.

You can never stop creating and trying new Diet Watchers dishes. It's as true for me as for you. I have been a slim person since 1961 and today I have to eat fattening foods to stay at my ideal weight of 120 pounds. Still I keep looking for new cooking ideas that use the DW foods for my own table. I also keep concocting new dishes for my groups to make DW eating interesting for them. And by creating these new recipes I have kept interested in the foods myself.

It's natural to tire of foods even when they do wonderful things for you. Would you want to wear the same dress or suit all the time?

You may see that certain basic lines in clothing are always flattering for you. For a woman an A-line shift, for example, might do more for her figure than any other kind of dress. But wouldn't you get tired of wearing the A-line all the time, no matter how flattering its shape? Wouldn't you look for new colors, new decorative elements, new accessories for that basic dress, to keep up your interest in the line? The same is true for even the foods you love and that do wonderful things for your figure.

Take *steak*. Immediately, if you are like me, the word makes you see beef sizzling on the broiler. Yet if you keep on eating it only that way, even steak will get dull.

I am a food-aholic and I love steak. In my house when we were all taking off fat I served steak Tuesdays, Thursdays and Sundays. Friday nights I served chicken. That was a steady food pattern. But I never made the steak or chicken the same way twice in a row. I put the chicken on the rotisserie. Another night I marinated it. Then I glazed it. My family always sat down to dinner and said, "Oooh, what's this? They never said, "Ugh, chicken again!" The new ways of seasoning and cooking, the new look of the foods made them interesting each time.

One reason for getting bored with foods you eat the same way often is our need to have interest for the eye. Everyone needs this eye appeal in food but a fat person even more than a slim one just because a fat person lives to eat. Any food that has eye appeal will make a fat person want to eat it. So I have found that making Diet Watchers foods interesting to the eye is a secret of keeping a fat person on this healthy diet. (It's relatively easy on this program because you have so much variety in the foods themselves.)

The gourmet ideal is excellent for the diet watcher. The gourmet savors good food and is very different from the *gourmand* or glutton, who eats piggishly, mistaking quantity for quality. The gourmet appreciates *different* foods.

It's a good idea to explore the foods of different ethnic groups. Why stick only to the foods of your own ethnic background? The others introduce variety.

You'll find that if you begin to cook differently you gain a new sense of adventure in eating differently and even an impetus toward living differently. When you change your cooking you are being more creative than before and so it makes the "work" of cooking more fun, more satisfying to you just because you are not doing the same thing over and over.

When I was fat I lived a life of sameness. I thought the same way, shopped in the same stores, for the same foods, dressed the same way, looked the same way, cooked the same way day after day.

You think your family wants you to cook the same way? My family never knows today what I will offer next in our house. When they were all fat, they knew what they would eat, and the only thing that makes a fat person happy is food. But they are happier today than they every were before.

In this book we've gone "around the world" to find the national dishes so interesting they have been acclaimed by people of all ethnic groups as gourmet eating. We show you how to make these dishes into DW style meals, using the foods and portions that make you slim. The emphasis is on taste, variety, novelty, fun—the important psychological ingredients to good eating. The flavor of Paris's Champs-Elysees, London's Piccadilly Circus, the aromas of Budapest and Bombay (but not the fat) are what you'll find in this Diet Watchers cookbook.

A word about entertaining. (There's a whole section on entertaining inside.) Dieters are often afraid to entertain. They fear they'll set back their own diet program by weeks, or have to serve "uninteresting" food.

But many dishes here will give you the motif or main dish for a party, *and* advance your dieting, *and* get you compliments from your guests and a kiss from your husband.

Gone is the old idea of entertaining: to heap food on a visitor following the philosophy of conspicuous consumption to eating extremes. Today's figure-conscious guests resent it. They want a host or hostess to serve food that says, "I'm thinking of *you* and so here is tasty, healthy, diet-watching food.

The recipes you will find here will give you a reputation as a better cook. They are modern foods, today's dishes, prepared in the new ways. You won't find them in your grandmother's or mother's collection of recipes, or in last year's cookbook.

These are NOW foods. They're for the new youthful slim generations.

MAKE A PLAN TO LEARN
THIS NEW COOKING

Your kitchen techniques can help you succeed or fail in your diet program. Make a plan for your day's work that allows you the time to learn this cooking. Remember: People who start the day—any day—without a plan for it never get much done.

Never begin cooking until you've cleaned the rest of the house. The reason is simple. When other rooms in the house are dirty or even just still untidy, you'll be so worried about the jobs you have to do that you'll tend to let the new cooking slide. This order of business works for me:

1. The first thing I do on awakening is to dress and then eat breakfast—first, in other words, I take care of myself.

2. Next I clean the entire house so I'll have no worries about other household jobs while cooking.

3. Now I go into the kitchen and tidy up there. I work in a neat kitchen surrounded only by the utensils I need for the cooking I am about to do.

4. I read the recipe for what I plan to make.

5. I take out all containers with the ingredients I need.

6. I measure out the amounts I need, and put away as many packages as I can. I work only with the amounts I will actually be using. You'll be surprised how much easier and more fun it is to cook when the kitchen isn't cluttered up with anything but the cooking ingredients, in the amounts you actually want.

7. I combine and put up the foods to cook, following directions of the recipe.

WHAT YOU SHOULD KNOW ABOUT
EATING THE DIET WATCHERS WAY

Many experts have now come to agree with us that calorie counting to take off fat is a clumsy system, and hard for most people to maintain.

We don't count calories in the DW program. Instead, we use a structured plan that divides all foods into three kinds —unlimited, limited and forbidden. We also tell you exactly how much and when to eat each kind.

Our system allows you a tremendous variety of foods, and so it helps you to create a new eating pattern you can stay with and enjoy—while you achieve the slim figure you want.

The DW diet has nothing in common with crash or fad diets and it does not involve pills or exercise. If you enjoy exercise and sports for other reasons—fine! We aren't against exercise, but our diet doesn't depend on exercise. It slims you and maintains you on its own. You don't need extra vitamins with DW eating. Our plan is fully nutritious, possibly more so than your present fattening diet. The good nutrition comes from the variety of foods in it, and from the structured plan for eating.

Because it is structured, this is also an *easy* diet to keep. You soon learn which foods are unlimited, limited or taboo —and when you can have them.

You can obtain our foods easily in your regular stores to prepare at home, and just as easily in most restaurants, if you are selective when the waiter or waitress hands you the regular menu.

But to help you make the dishes in this cookbook properly, here is what you need to know about the basic Diet Watchers diet:

1. The Unlimited Foods. You may eat the following foods at any time of day, *in any quantity you want*, with any meal—or alone as a snack. Look up the recipes for preparing them in many different appetizing ways. Add them to any full course meal if you need more food. Don't over-eat with them if you don't have to, but use them to keep you from eating the fattening foods:

asparagus	mushrooms
bean sprouts	mustard greens
beat greens	parsley
broccoli	pickles
cabbage	pimientos
cauliflower	radishes

celery
Chinese cabbage
cucumber
endive
escarole
green & red pepper
lettuce

sauerkraut
spinach
summer squash
string beans (French-style
  only)
watercress

Also unlimited are these seasonings and sauces:

horseradish
mustard
lemon
pepper
paprika

salt
vinegar
all other spices
all herbs (oregano, thyme,
garlic, etc.)

These drinks are also anytime, unlimited drinks, except for the tomato juice, which you may have any time of day but only in the amount of 8 ounces during the day:

> bouillon
> carbonated beverages (non-caloric kind only)
> clear soups (fat free only)
> coffee (black, with non-sugar sweetener)
> lemon and lime drinks (without sugar)
> seltzer or club soda
> tea
> tomato juice (8 ounces only)
> water

2. Limited Foods. You may eat one serving of a *Limited Vegetable*—at dinnertime only—each day. The amount is limited to *four ounces* of:

LIMITED VEGETABLES

artichokes
bamboo shoots
beets
Brussels sprouts
carrots
eggplant
green beans (mature)
okra
onions

oyster plant
parsnips
peas
pumpkin
scallions
squash
  (acorn, butternut, etc.)
tomato
turnips

Vary your selection from day to day. Try new vegetables from this list you haven't used before. You can combine any two or more if you want, as long as the total serving from this list weighs no more than four ounces.

FRUITS

You *must have* three fruits every day if you are a woman, and men should have four. At least one daily fruit should be a high Vitamin C fruit such as orange or grapefruit. You may eat any fruit *except* bananas, cherries, watermelon, dried fruits or grapes.

MEATS, FISH AND POULTRY

Eat from the following three times weekly:

beefsteak	liver
frankfurters	steak
lamb	roast beef
fresh salmon	hamburger
turkey—dark meat	

For all other meals during the week, you choose from the following meats and fish:

FIRST CHOICE

abalone	lobster
bass	lungs
brains	mussels
chicken (breast)	oysters
cod	pike
finnan haddie	scallops
flounder	shrimp
haddock	sturgeon (fresh only)
heart (beef)	trout (brook)
kidney	weakfish

SECOND CHOICE

bluefish	shad
bonito	shad roe
butterfish	swordfish
chicken	trout (lake)
eels	tuna (fresh or canned,
kidney (beef)	waterpacked)
mackerel	turkey (light meat only)
pheasant	veal
rabbit	whitefish
salmon (canned)	

Other general rules for meats, fish and poultry are:

Eat at least five fish or seafood meals weekly.

Broil, bake or roast only. Never fry in fat.

Trim off all visible fat before eating.

Don't use gravies or sauces except those made with DW recipes.

3. Bread

Women *must* eat one slice of enriched white bread each day at breakfast, and a second slice at lunch. Men (and teen boys) may have two slices at each of those meals.

4. Eggs

You may eat from four to seven eggs a week. It may be cooked in the shell, poached, or Teflon-scrambled, but without butter or other fat. You will find a number of unusual and tempting egg recipes in this book.

5. Milk

You *must* drink two glasses (16 ounces total) of skim milk or buttermilk every day—no more, no less. Have it anytime, any way you like—at or between meals, as a drink, dressing, or part of a recipe. Make skim milk from non-fat dry solids rather than using the liquid kind. For better taste, chill in the refrigerator overnight before drinking.

6. THE TABOO FOODS

Until you reach your diet goal do not eat or drink any of the following:

alcoholic beverages (straight or mixed)	French fried potatoes	sugar
	fried foods	syrups
	gefilte fish	nuts
beer, wine, whiskey	(except for the DW version	oil
avocado	you'll find in	olives
bacon (*or any fat*)	this book)	pancakes
butter	gravy	peanut butter
cake	honey	pies
candy	ice cream	popcorn
chocolate	jam	potato chips
coconut	jelly	pretzels
cookies	Jello	puddings
crackers	ketchup	salad dressings
cream (sweet or sour)	mayonnaise	soda
doughnuts	muffins	ginger ale
French dressing	smoked fish	cola drinks
		waffles
		yogurt
		ices

7. The Rest of the Diet Watcher Rules

1. *See your doctor first.*

Many physicians send patients to our Diet Watchers groups because their fat has begun to threaten health. Heart and diabetic patients are among them. *However, Diet Watchers does not accept new members who have a health problem without a doctor's written approval. Wheth-er or not you have a health problem you should not put yourself on any diet without such protection.*

2. *Don't deviate.* Don't add, substitute or subtract. Every "*must*" food in the diet is vital for your health and good appearance.

3. *Don't skip meals.* If you try to "get ahead" this way, you'll get too famished to exercise the control you need to stay on the diet. We don't allow more than five hours between meals and we eat breakfast no more than one hour after awakening.

4. *Measure all foods exactly.* We use an eight-ounce glass; four-ounce half-cup; four-ounce dinner vegetable portion; three-ounce lunch and six-ounce dinner portions for meat, fish and poultry, unless otherwise noted.

Buy one of those small inexpensive and marvelous diet helps, a postage scale. It costs only three or four dollars, shows weight by ounces and teaches you the correct portion sizes. Use an aluminum dish to hold the food you are weighing and weigh your portions after cooking, as you serve. Allowing two ounces more for raw meat (and for fish with bones and skin) generally gives you the correct ounce portion after cooking.

5. Eat foods only at the time or meal of day specified: bread *only* at breakfast and lunch, the limited vegetable at dinner. Study the menu plans in "Two Weeks Around the World" to see how the dishes are combined into a nutritious eating pattern. Actually, we rearrange the pattern to suit individual needs in DW groups so that each person loses pounds faster. This is not possible in a book. But the general pattern given here will enable you to lose fat consistently until you reach your goal.

6. *Weigh yourself once a week.* Choose the same time of day, use a good scale, and wear about the same amount of clothes. Keep a record of your weekly weight (use the worksheets in the back of this book to catch your errors or cheating).

YOU HAVE TO HAVE A SYSTEM

When a fat person worries that DW cooking takes time, I ask: "How do you go about preparing the food in your house? What's your system?"

Anyone who lives without system is disorganized. You have to live with a system not only for diet but to accomplish anything. A system let's you do all the things you have to do and helps you to lead a fuller, richer life. There is a saying: "If you want something done quickly, give it to a busy person. He'll *make time* to fit it into the schedule and still relax." It's true.

When I first went on my diet I was working fulltime. I had to devise a system so that I could work and prepare the proper food. Every minute had to count. I devised my plan then of always cooking at night for the next night.

When I came home from work, I prepared dinner (actually this had been cooked the night before unless it was a broiled food), and we all ate. Then I cleared the table and counters and stacked the used dishes and utensils in the sink.

I was ready now for everyone's next day lunches. Working on the cleaned counter, I made four lunches, packed them in paper bags marked for each person and put them into the refrigerator. I then cooked dinner for the next night. When this was done I was ready to wash the dishes and clean the kitchen.

MY SYSTEM TODAY

My days now are very busy. I give three long lectures each day, one each in the morning, afternoon and night. I will tell you my present dinnertime program because it shows how much you can do when you work out a clear system.

I arrive home from my afternoon group lecture at 3:30 p.m. and allow myself one hour to do shopping or chores. Then I undress, take my kitchen timer into the bedroom and set it to ring in 25 minutes, just as though I were cooking. I move the telephone out of my bedroom, take a quick hot shower, shut my bedroom door and get into bed.

My family knows I need this. I've insisted they know it is *my* time. (A mother teaches her family this way. My husband and children have also learned to take a half hour rest as their time during the day.) Anyway, I love this time of my own. I am in night clothes, truly relaxing. I've been working hard every minute since early morning and now I can virtually feel the sparks of the day escaping, and my body simmering down. Sometimes I doze off, sometimes I don't . . .

When the timer goes off I get up, put on a housedress, go into the kitchen and prepare the dinner. While it's cooking I dress for my evening lecture.

Five p.m. is dinnertime in my house. It might be a different hour in yours but that is the necessity in our home and everyone knows it. We are done in about half an hour and we all enjoy dinner. We talk about school, funny happenings of the day, whatever. Our meals are happy meals. We eat *something* fancy every night of the week, something exciting or new, something different.

HOW I COOK TODAY

I have a six-day working schedule, so my own program today may be different from yours. I cook for the whole week on weekends, in bulk, and I freeze meals. Those fifteen minutes I spend each evening preparing dinner usually are to cook vegetables, to warm any roasted meats I have defrosted, or to broil.

This system—cooking on the weekend—lets me experiment and take time when I have it and gives me the *quick proper* meals during my busy weekdays. But I have always followed a similar plan. I never cooked dinner meals the same night I planned to serve them.

When the children were small, before I went out to work, I planned my week so I did the laundry one day, the ironing another, some heavy cleaning the third, and so on. I cooked for the week every Friday. The system gave me more time with my children and an organized week. When I went on the Diet Watchers program I had plenty of time to learn the proper cooking and to experiment with new dishes, and it was useful to have meals prepared for the busy days.

OTHER SYSTEMS

Maybe long-range cooking is wrong for you. Try arranging your day so you *cook in the morning* for each night, instead of just before dinner. You'll be more likely to try new ideas. When you cook just before dinner you are always aware of the pressure of time and you can be pushed to fall back on the old cooking habits you already know well, rather than experiment with a new recipe or new technique. It does take a few minutes to learn to brown in a Teflon pot or in the oven, instead of in your usual frypan with fat.

Try making two dinners at a time—one to have that night, another to freeze. If you have a freezer, it can be a great help. You can freeze just about every Diet Watchers dish.

THE SECRET OF DW ONE POT COOKING

My one pot DW cooking was, as I admit, a holdover from when I was fat. When I began to experiment with the DW foods I wanted to keep my one pot cooking and devised tricks to use one large pot for several ingredients of a meal. If you want to stew several fruits in one pot, for example, tear a piece of heavy gauge aluminum foil twice the diameter, or width, of the pot. Fold it down the center to create a center wall. That gives you separate compartments. Let both fruits cook in the same liquid, and you save cleaning one pot.

DO YOU HAVE THE ENERGY?

"But it takes such a long time to prepare the food!" fat people often tell me.

That is not true. It's just an excuse you are setting up because *you don't want to make the change.* A fat person always wants things easy. To work is an effort. But I have energy now to do many things I could not do when I was younger—and fat.

Last Christmas I went to buy something in a variety store and just as I was about to open the door a huge women came out. She was tall and just tremendously fat, heaving and breathing hard as though she carried a weight on her chest. I guessed she was only in her thirties, but her hard breathing stopped me—she was *suffocating*. "Excuse me!" I said on impulse. "Please don't be angry! I want to tell you something. . ."

Then I realized she was a total stranger and could send me flying through space. She saw the fear in my face. She said, looking down at me, "Why? Is my slip showing?"

"No!" (I thought, "It's your fat that's showing," but I stopped myself this time). "No, your slip isn't showing. But I don't know how to tell you."

"—My *panties?"* Now she looked horrified.

"Oh no, no!" I said. "But would you believe *I* was fat just a short time ago?"

She calmed down. "Really?" She considered my figure. "What happened? Were you sick?"

I pointed across the street to our offices where a Diet Watchers sign could be seen in a window. It says, "Lose ugly fat. No pills. No counting calories. Eat Your Way Slim."

"I joined Diet Watchers," I told her.

"What is it? What did you do?" she asked.

I said it was just reeducating your way of eating. "Would you believe I now eat more than I ever did before in my life, and I lost 65 pounds?"

"Really?" She sounded amazed. "Are you still eating that way?"

"Now that I'm slim, I'm on maintenance."

"What's that?"

"I am now slim, and I can eat fattening foods properly, and still maintain my proper weight."

"Really?" It seemed to be all she could say.

"Wouldn't it be nice, next Christmas, to be slim, attractive, healthy and *sexy?*"

"I'll take health!" she said immediately.

"Come to our group Monday morning," I urged her.

She came and she lost twelve pounds in her very first week. The second week she lost 5 ½ pounds—she had dropped down two dress sizes.

What had stopped me the first time I saw her? That although she was only in her thirties, she had to struggle for breath to walk through a store door!

Energy? I became a grandmother that same holiday— my daughter Sharyn had her first baby. It was during a severe epidemic of Hong Kong flu and because of it the hospital would not allow me to visit. I had worked at that hospital as a volunteer and knew there were back stairs up to the nursery floor. Like any impatient grandmother I sneaked up the back way and looked through the upstairs nursery window as a nurse took a newborn baby off the scale. She was wrapping its long black hair around her finger to make it into a curl. I tapped the glass. She held the baby up. It was my grandchild! I jumped up and down and they came and threw me out.

That same holiday I also learned how to *roller skate* with my younger, twelve-year-old daughter. It was wonderful! (I had learned how to ice skate, *for the first time in my life,* only the year before.) I have no energy problems, and I am a grandmother. Yet I had never roller skated as a kid—I was too fat. Maybe that's why skating is so much fun for me now, because I never did it as a kid. I still keep realizing what being fat did to me. It robbed me of more than energy. I always felt I was missing so much of life because of my fat.

Anyway, going to "extra" trouble with new dishes will *not* use up energy you need. The truth is, making these new dishes will give you more energy than you ever dreamed possible.

WHY FUSS?

Many people, especially fat people, panic when they read recipes. They don't realize that reading the recipe is actually half the job of cooking a new dish!

So much depends on your mental attitude. There is fear about new foods. I remember how the idea of using powders to make skim milk and for other 'ingredients panicked me when I first began cooking this new way. Today I work with powders without even thinking. There's nothing strange or fearful or complicated about them. You will do the same.

When fat people tell me that cooking healthful meals means "fussing," I tell them the real problem is a certain meagerness of thought that is typical of the fat person. She doesn't want to spend much time preparing a meal because *she gets no pleasure in the cooking*. So she panics over "fussing."

The truth is, when I fussed, I made fried foods. This is the kind of cooking that actually needs fussing.

When I first began DW cooking I visualized my kitchen as a mess of dirty pots. The idea scared me. Then I found that the cooking was actually *simpler*.

DW cooking is not difficult cooking. It is not even different cooking. It is only different *thinking*. All the steps are simple, and there are no fancy techniques, no *mystiques* here. You use less utensils than you did before, often only one pot. (When I was fat I made fattening meals just because I wanted to cook in one pot.)

LIFE CAN BE SIMPLER

This new cooking makes your entire life simpler. Shopping for food becomes simpler. Other kinds of shopping as well—shopping for clothes, for example. When I was fat, nothing I tried on looked good to me or on me. Now everything looks good. Buying clothes is easy and fun. Now my husband is so excited about how clothes look on me that he doesn't ask how much I spent. That makes life simpler, too!

AROUND THE WORLD GOURMET RECIPES
(Breakfasts, lunches, dinners . . . main dishes, vegetables, side dishes, salads, sauces)

RECIPE ARRANGEMENT

These Diet Watchers recipes are arranged by country to take you around the world. We go east, toward Europe first, and stop off at the lands with the most popular cooking. Within each country, to help you with your diet watching program, the recipes follow a day's eating: That is, breakfasts start the day, then come lunches, and finally dinners. All the soups, side dishes, snacks and sauces, in that order, follow the dinners.

SALT

Diet Watchers recipes are not for ill people, only for those who want to become slim, so they include all foods but the fattening ones.

However, you may notice that in some recipes, salt is given as an optional ingredient. If you prefer, you can drop the salt from *any* recipe here, just as you can (and *should*) experiment after awhile, to adapt the amounts of seasoning in any recipe to your own personal taste.

BUTTER FLAVORING

A number of recipes, especially among Italian dishes, list butter flavoring among the ingredients. This is almost always optional. You may prefer the dish with smaller amounts than suggested, or even without this taste. If you can't find imitation butter flavoring where you live, in most cases you can use the same recipe without it.

THE ITALIAN HAND

BREAKFAST

SPARAGI CHEESE BREAKFAST
(Breakfast only)

⅛ teaspoon imitation
butter flavoring
1 slice white bread
1 can asparagus, drained

Salt and pepper to taste
1 ounce Swiss or Muen-
ster cheese
Dash parsley

Swirl butter flavoring in a baking dish to coat it. Toast bread lightly and place in baking dish, covering it with the asparagus. Add salt and pepper, then top with cheese and garnish with parsley. Broil far from flame just until cheese melts and turns slightly brown.

This recipe is one breakfast serving.

LUNCH

HOT GARLIC BREAD
(Lunch only)

1 slice white bread
Garlic powder

Few drops imitation
butter flavoring

Sprinkle the bread liberally with garlic powder on both sides. Add a few drops of butter flavoring, then toast lightly.

ITALIAN PASTAS

..The Italians are a wonderful, warm friendly people. And you'd think God created Sunday just for eating cheating! ... Italian women think they *must* make pasta for their husbands, to keep their love. In the kitchen, there's no denying, a dish of pasta looks delightful. But on a fat woman it looks—like pasta! Here's a way to make DW pasta and look delicious:

PASTA FLOWERETTES
(Lunch only)

1 head cauliflower
⅓ cup dry milk powder
2 ounces sliced Swiss or
Muenster cheese

¼ cup tomato juice
Parsley
Oregano
½ teaspoon garlic powder

Wash cauliflower and break into flowerettes, any size you like. Cook about 15 minutes, until tender. Dip damp

27

flowerettes into dry milk powder (use a bowl). Place flowerettes in a casserole, cut cheese into narrow strips and crisscross the top like lattice work. Combine tomato juice, parsley, oregano and garlic powder and pour the mixture over the dish. Bake in 325° oven until cheese melts and starts to brown. *Ciao!* Pasta!

For more "pasta" shapes that are fun, try using asparagus stalks or broccoli instead of cauliflowerettes.

This equals one lunch main dish serving and one glass of milk.

SCALLOPS SCAMPI

½ teaspoon garlic powder	Oregano
3 ounces tomato juice	4 ounces scallops
½ teaspoon parsley flakes	1 can bean sprouts
Paprika	1 can mushrooms

Combine the garlic powder, tomato juice, parsley flakes and dashes of paprika and oregano in a bowl. Marinate the scallops in this sauce 2 hours. Line your broiler with foil, turning the ends up to hold the sauce. Place scallops and sauce in this and broil on each side 5 minutes, or until tender. Heat sprouts and mushrooms, drain well, combine them and put the mix on a platter. Top with the scallops and sauce.

This is a seafood lunch serving and three ounces of tomato juice.

DINNERS

CAESAR'S VEAL

8 ounces lean veal, trimmed well and cubed	3 ounces plum tomatoes, halved
Garlic powder	¼ cup tomato juice
¼ teaspoon white pepper	1 tablespoon parsley
2 green peppers cut in strips	⅛ teaspoon oregano
⅛ ounce onion, diced	

Place veal cubes in Teflon pan, sprinkle heavily with garlic powder and white pepper and brown them. When almost brown, add the pepper strips and onion. When all browned, add the tomatoes, tomato juice, parsley and oregano. Cover and simmer ¾ hour, until meat is tender. If liquid cooks out, add another ¼ cup tomato juice. Refrigerate. Skim off fat and reheat to serve.

This recipe equals a dinner meat serving, a dinner vegetable and two ounces of tomato juice.

CHICKEN AND ANTIPASTO

6 ounces cooked chicken
(or turkey white meat)

Antipasto DW

Cut cooked chicken or turkey white meat into thick ½ inch strips. Marinate overnight in the pickling marinade used for Antipasto vegetables (see index). Put Antipasto on platter and top with the marinated chicken to make a complete dinner.

The platter equals a dinner serving and a dinner vegetable.

CHICKEN CACCIATORE

2 ½ -pound chicken, quartered	4 ounces tomato juice
4 ounces onion, chopped	1 bay leaf, crushed
2 cloves garlic, diced	¼ pound fresh mushrooms
¼ teaspoon paprika	or 1 can drained
¼ teaspoon oregano	2 green peppers, in strips
	1 can bean sprouts

Remove skin from chicken, break away the wings and drumsticks and season chicken with paprika and oregano. In a covered Teflon frypan, simmer the onion and garlic 5 minutes. Lay chicken over the onion and brown both over high flame. Add tomato juice, bay leaf, mushrooms, pepper strips and more oregano, cover and simmer 1 hour. Let cool. Refrigerate and skim off fat. Reheat to serve. Pour all the sauce over half the chicken. Or reserve the sauce to pour over DW spaghetti (see index).

This recipe is a dinner serving plus two ounces of dinner vegetable and two ounces of tomato juice.

CHICKEN OREGANO

1 broiler (3 pounds)	1 clove garlic, chopped
Salt and pepper, to taste	⅛ cup imitation butter
2 teaspoons oregano	flavoring (optional)
¼ cup lemon juice	1 teaspoon parsley

Clean and quarter the broiler and sprinkle lightly with salt and pepper. In a small bowl, combine the oregano, lemon juice, garlic, butter flavoring and parsley, then brush chicken generously with this mixture. Broil chicken skin side up, 6 inches from high flame, about 20 minutes on each side (until brown and tender). Brush occasionally with liquid mixture to prevent dryness. Half a chicken is one dinner serving.

CHICKEN ROMANO

Half a 2 ½ pound
broiler, cut as for frying
¼ teaspoon paprika
¼ teaspoon oregano
Parsley

2 ounces onion, sliced
2 ounces tomato, peeled
and sliced
1 box frozen summer
squash, or 1 pound fresh

Brown chicken under broiler so that fat drips down into the pan (10 minutes on each side). Chicken will be partly done. Remove and pat dry with paper towel. Sprinkle with paprika, oregano, parsley. Place in roasting pan and add onion, tomato and squash. Dust a bit more oregano on top and bake in 350° oven 1 hour.

This recipe is a dinner serving and one dinner vegetable.

CHICKEN WITH MUSHROOMS

1 broiler (3 pounds)
Salt
Pepper
Parsley
Oregano
Garlic powder

⅛ teaspoon imitation
butter flavoring
1 large onion, sliced
2 cloves garlic
1 pound fresh mushrooms
2 tablespoons water

Cut chicken as for frying and wash and dry thoroughly. Sprinkle lightly with salt, pepper, parsley, oregano, garlic powder. Heat butter flavoring in large Teflon frypan and add the garlic cloves and chicken, browning it on both sides (about 10 minutes). Lower flame, cover tightly and continue cooking 25 minutes. Add onion, mushrooms and the water, re-cover tightly and simmer 30 to 40 minutes, until chicken is tender. If water cooks out, add a little at a time.

Half the chicken is one dinner serving.

EGGPLANT STUFFED WITH VEAL

½ pound ground veal
Pepper
Paprika
⅛ teaspoon garlic powder

Pinch oregano
½ cup tomato juice
1 medium eggplant

To the ground veal add a dash of pepper, paprika, the garlic powder, oregano and half the tomato juice. Mix well and set aside. Halve the eggplant lengthwise, but do not peel it. Scoop out the center and dice this very fine. Weigh off 4 ounces and mix this portion with the veal. Fill eggplant shells with the veal-eggplant stuffing. Place in a baking dish with the rest of the tomato juice. Cover each stuffed egg-plant with foil, sealing foil all around at the top. Bake 1 hour in a preheated 325° oven, then remove the foil and bake another half hour. If tomato juice cooks out, add a bit more.

This is a dinner meat serving, a dinner vegetable and four ounces of tomato juice.

PEPPERS STUFFED WITH "ITALIAN" SAUSAGE

4 large green peppers
8 ounces kosher style "Special" franks (the fat ones)
1 ounce onion, chopped fine
1 clove garlic, diced fine
¼ cup parsley flakes

Pepper to taste
1 chicken bouillon cube dissolved in ½ cup hot water
2 tablespoons tomato juice
DW rice

Cut tops off the peppers and scoop out insides completely. In a large pot, bring water to boil. Add peppers, reduce flame and simmer 3 minutes to soften them slightly. Remove and let cool. Remove casing from "Special" franks and dice the meat into a Teflon pan. Add the onion and garlic and brown 10 minutes. Stir while browning. Mix well with parsley and pepper and stuff mixture into green pepper shells. Combine chicken bouillon and tomato juice in a casserole. Arrange stuffed peppers in this liquid, cover and bake in preheated 350° oven 25 minutes. Add 1 portion of DW rice, bake another 5 minutes and serve.

This recipe equals a dinner beef serving, one ounce of a dinner vegetable and two tablespoons of tomato juice.

ROASTED RABBIT

1 rabbit, 3 to 4 pounds
2 tablespoons salt
1 teaspoon imitation butter flavoring
2 medium onions, chopped

Dash salt
⅛ teaspoon crushed red pepper seeds
2 tomatoes, quartered
4 carrots, sliced
1 cup water

Have rabbit cleaned and cut into serving pieces. Place in pot with water to cover, add salt and let stand 2 hours. Then wash in cold running water and dry with paper towel. Sauté in large covered Teflon pan with butter flavoring, onion, salt and red pepper seeds for 20 minutes. Remove cover, raise flame and brown. Add tomatoes and carrots. Cover tightly and cook on low flame 20 minutes. Add the water and continue cooking ½ hour or until rabbit and carrots are tender.

Six ounces of rabbit equal one dinner portion and 4 ounces of vegetables are one dinner vegetable.

SHRIMP SCAMPI

10 ounces shrimp in shell	Dash salt
4 garlic cloves	Pepper
6 ounces tomato juice	Paprika
½ teaspoon parsley flakes	Dash oregano

Shell, wash and devein the shrimp. Make the sauce: Crush the garlic cloves and mix with the tomato juice in a medium sized bowl; add parsley flakes, salt, dashes of pepper and oregano. Marinate uncooked shrimp in this seasoned sauce 2 hours. Line broiler with aluminum foil, turning up the sides, and when shrimp has marinated, place them on the foil. Pour marinade over them. Broil shrimp 5 minutes on each side. Serve them with any marinade left over and with cooked broccoli or cauliflower.

This is one dinner seafood serving and 6 ounces of tomato juice.

SPAGHETTI DW STYLE AND MEAT BALLS

½ pound chopped beef	1 small can mushrooms, drained
6 ounces tomato juice	
Oregano	1 can La Choy
½ teaspoon garlic powder	bean sprouts,
½ teaspoon parsley	drained

To the chopped beef add 2 ounces of the tomato juice, a dash of oregano and garlic powder and mix well. Wet hands with cold water and roll meat into small balls. Broil 5 minutes on each side, just to brown. Drain off the fat. In a sauce pan combine the rest of the tomato juice, rest of the garlic powder, the parsley and another dash of oregano and bring to a boil. Gently add the meat balls to the boiling sauce. Simmer, 1 hour, covered. Cool. Refrigerate and skim off all fat. Reheat thoroughly to serve, adding the mushrooms and bean sprouts. Place bean sprouts on serving platter first and top with the meat balls, and the sauce.

This recipe is a dinner beef serving and 6 ounces of tomato juice.

SWEET AND SOUR SQUASH

2 large zucchini	3 tablespoons wine vinegar
½ teaspoon imitation butter flavoring	
	1 tablespoon chopped sweet basil
Salt and pepper to taste	½ teaspoon parsley flakes
2 to 3 drops liquid non-sugar sweetener	

Wash and scrub the zucchini thoroughly with a brush to remove any sand. Cut into lengthwise slices, 3/8 inches thick. Put into a Teflon pan with the butter flavoring and brown lightly on each side. Add salt and pepper. Cover and simmer 5 minutes (just until tender). Transfer to serving dish. For sauce: Leave butter flavoring in pan, add sweetener and the vinegar, cover and simmer 2 minutes. Pour over the zucchini, and top with sweet basil and parsley.

Four ounces equal a dinner vegetable.

VENISON ROAST

2 cups vinegar
4 cups cold water
2 large carrots, sliced
2 cloves garlic, diced
2 tablespoons parsley

2 whole cloves
2 large onions, sliced
4 pounds venison
Salt and pepper, to taste

Combine the vinegar and water and bring to a boil. Remove from heat and add the carrots, one sliced onion, garlic, parsley and cloves. Let cool. Marinate venison in this mixture in a cold place about 24 hours. Remove venison, dry with paper toweling and sprinkle it with salt and pepper. Place second sliced onion and venison in a baking pan and brown venison in 350° oven about 30 minutes (turn to prevent burning). Then add all the marinating vegetables and enough marinade to make a gravy, and lower heat to 325°. Roast, basting occasionally with the marinade 1 ½ hours (or until venison is tender). Serve hot.

Six ounces of venison are a dinner beef serving and 4 ounces of carrot and onion equal a dinner vegetable.

VENISON STEAKS

2 cups vinegar
4 cups cold water
1 onion, diced
1 carrot, diced
4 pounds venison

Salt and pepper, to taste
Parsley flakes
Pimiento

Mix the vinegar and water in a saucepan and bring to a boil. Remove from heat. Add the onion and carrot and let cool. Marinate venison in the cooled mixture in a cold place 24 hours. Then slice venison into steaks and season with salt, pepper and parsley flakes. Broil far from flame (in preheated broiler) as you would steak. Venison must be well done. Serve with pimiento.

Six ounces of venison are a dinner beef serving. The carrot and onion equal one dinner vegetable.

ANTIPASTO

1 romaine lettuce
   Summer squash, washed
   well and sliced
   paper thin
* Marinated French-style
   string beans (see recipe)
1 ounce large onion,
   sliced thin,
   separated into rings
* Marinated
   cauliflowerettes
   Green and red sweet
   pepper, cut into strips

* Marinated broccoli
   spears
* Marinated asparagus
   spears
4 or 5 stalks celery
4 or 5 stalks
   Chinese cabbage
10 whole red radishes
   Red pimientos
   Cucumber, sliced
   diagonally (do not peel)
*1 ounce pickled beets
2 ounces tomato

*See Index for all starred ingredients. Tear lettuce into eating pieces and crisp 10 minutes in a mixing bowl half filled with ice cubes. Transfer to large platter. Top with marinated vegetables, then with the other ingredients. Pour DW Italian garlic vinegar over all.

This entire recipe equals one dinner vegetable.

BOILED ESCAROLE
(Unlimited)

2 pounds escarole   Dash salt
1 clove garlic, diced

Discard tough or faded outer leaves, and separate the rest. Wash thoroughly, then boil in water to cover, seasoned with the garlic and with salt to taste 20 minutes, or until tender. Drain well. Chop and serve.

ESCAROLE SALAD
(Unlimited)

1 medium head escarole
2 tablespoons wine
   vinegar
¼ teaspoon imitation
   butter flavoring

4 leaves fresh sweet
   basil, chopped
   Salt and pepper
   to taste

Discard outside escarole leaves. Wash thoroughly and crisp in ice water about 15 minutes. Drain well and pat dry with paper towel, cut into one inch pieces and transfer to salad bowl. In a small carafe, mix the wine vinegar, butter flavoring, basil, salt and pepper to taste. Pour over the greens and toss well.

SAUTEED ESCAROLE
(Unlimited)

2 pounds escarole
⅛ teaspoon imitation butter flavoring

1 clove garlic diced
Parsley flakes

Discard tough or faded outer leaves, then separate the rest of the escarole and wash thoroughly. Drain and cut leaves in half. Heat butter flavoring in large Teflon frypan and brown the garlic in it. Add escarole. Cook over medium flame, covered, 20 minutes or until tender. If it needs more liquid, add some chicken bouillon. Serve hot, topped with parsley flakes.

FAGIOLINI SAUTE

1 clove garlic, diced
¼ teaspoon imitation butter flavoring
1 large can French-style string beans

Salt and pepper to taste
Parsley

Brown the garlic in a large Teflon frypan, with the butter flavoring. Add drained string beans, salt and pepper, and toss. Cover and heat 5 minutes. Serve hot, topped with parsley.

LEMON FENNEL (FINOCCHIO)
(Unlimited)

1 bunch fennel Garlic-vinegar dressing

½ fresh lemon

Wash fennel well and slice into thin finger strips, including the roots. Steam until just tender. Cool, then marinate in DW garlic-vinegar dressing. Squeeze some fresh lemon juice over it and serve.

FRIED ITALIAN PEPPERS
(Unlimited)

2 Peppers
¼ cup tomato juice
1 tablespoon parsley

½ teaspoon garlic powder
Pinch oregano

Wash peppers, cut them in half and remove seeds. Place in Teflon frypan with the tomato juice, parsley, garlic powder and oregano. Cover and simmer until peppers are tender (10 to 15 minutes).

An anytime, as well as unlimited food.

Or, for a variation you will like: Add 1 can mushrooms, 1 can bean sprouts and 1 can French-style string beans, all heated and well drained.

GARLIC VEGETABLE DISH
(Unlimited)

1 can French style
   string beans
1 can mushrooms

1 can bean sprouts
Black pepper
Garlic powder

Combine and heat the string beans, mushrooms and bean sprouts. Drain. Sprinkle heavily with black pepper and garlic powder, mixing well. Serve.

GARLIC-VINEGAR DRESSING
(Unlimited)

1 cup white vinegar

4 cloves garlic, peeled
   and halved

In a small pot heat vinegar to boiling point. Remove from heat, add garlic. Allow to stand one hour, then remove garlic. Pour into stoppered bottle or covered jar and refrigerate. Delicious over salads.

ITALIAN EGGPLANT WITH MUSHROOM STUFFING

1 large eggplant
1 pound fresh mush-
   rooms, sliced
1 onion, chopped
1 teaspoon parsley flakes

Dash garlic powder
Oregano
Paprika
2 tablespoons tomato
   juice

Cut eggplant in half lengthwise, and with a curved grapefruit knife, scoop out some of the pulp. Save pulp but discard the center seeds. Steam shell and pulp in double boiler until shell is flexible but not soft. Set shell aside. Place mushrooms in half the Teflon frypan; in other half arrange eggplant pulp and the onion. Cover and cook over low flame 10 minutes (until mushrooms are soft). Remove from heat. Combine pulp, mushrooms and onion with parsley, garlic powder, oregano, paprika and the tomato juice, mixing well. Fill shells with this mixture. Serve on pretty platter.

One-half eggplant is a dinner vegetable.

ITALIAN EGGPLANT-ZUCCHINI SURPRISE

1 eggplant, medium or small	Paprika
	Parsley
1 large zucchini squash	Oregano
5 or 6 onions, sliced	½ teaspoon garlic powder
2 green peppers, in strips	⅓ cup tomato juice

Peel and cut the eggplant into ½-inch slices. Wash the zucchini well and cut into ½-inch slices. In a large covered Teflon pan cook the onion slices and pepper strips without water ten minutes or until soft, then remove the cover, raise flame and stir them as they brown. Dust the eggplant and zucchini with paprika, parsley, oregano and garlic powder. Cook in the tomato juice 10 minutes or until soft but not mushy. Drain well. Combine with the onion, green peas, mixing well, heat and serve.

Four ounces equal an unforgettable dinner vegetable!

MARINATED GARLIC EGGPLANT

1 medium eggplant	Lettuce
DW Italian garlic vinegar dressing	Sweet basil, chopped
	Red or green pepper
1 teaspoon oregano	strips
1 teaspoon chopped parsley	

Cut medium eggplant into ½ inch cubes. Steam in Teflon pan without water, covered, until tender but firm. Transfer to bowl and cover with the Italian dressing while still hot, adding oregano and parsley. Let stand 1 hour and serve on a bed of lettuce sprinkled with chopped basil and strips of green or red peppers. Delicious with lamb or beef. Any left over can be stored in a covered jar in the refrigerator.

Four ounces are a dinner vegetable.

PEPPERONI
(Unlimited)

10 large red peppers	1 tablespoon vinegar
1 clove garlic diced, or	Pinch oregano
½ teaspoon garlic powder	½ teaspoon parsley
	Salt and pepper
⅛ teaspoon imitation butter flavoring	to taste

Wash and dry the whole peppers. Broil 6 inches below medium flame 10 minutes on each side to brown and soften, but turn to avoid burning. When peppers are soft, remove and let cool. Peel off browned skin, open and remove seeds. Cut lengthwise into 2 inch strips. Make sauce: Combine all the other ingredients, mixing well. Place peppers in a deep dish and pour the sauce over them. Marinate in refrigerator until ready to serve. These are excellent cold with meat or fish.

Yes, unlimited! Use this even as a TV snack.

ROMAN SALAD
(Dinner Only)

3 or 4 red radishes
1 medium head romaine lettuce
1 cucumber, sliced thin diagonally
4 ounces sweet onion, sliced and broken into onion rings

2 tablespoons wine vinegar
⅛ teaspoon imitation butter flavoring
Salt and pepper, to taste
Parsley

Slice radishes lengthwise ¾ through (make about 4 slices per radish) and let stand in ice water 10 to 15 minutes or until they open like rosettes. Crisp lettuce in cold water*. Cut into 1 inch strips and place in salad bowl with cucumber and onion rings, and toss lightly. For the dressing, combine the vinegar, salt, pepper and butter flavoring. Pour over the greens and toss lightly. Then garnish with radish rosettes on top and sprinkle with some parsley.

*FAST WAY TO CRISP A SALAD: Empty a tray of ice cubes from freezer into a glass bowl. Stir until bowl is chilled, then add 1 glass cold water. Let stand 5 minutes, then add greens.

This equals one dinner vegetable.

SPAGHETTI—DW STYLE

1 can La Choy bean sprouts, drained well
Paprika
½ teaspoon garlic powder

Parsley
Dash oregano
2 tablespoons tomato juice

Combine all ingredients in a saucepan and simmer five minutes. Drain well and serve.

This equals two tablespoons of tomato juice.

FRENCH DELICACIES

BREAKFASTS

FRENCH CROISSANT
(Breakfast only)

1 slice enriched white bread	2 or 3 drops liquid non-sugar sweetener
1 egg	
⅛ teaspoon (optional) imitation butter flavoring	

Cut off bread crust, then cut slice into 2 triangles. On aluminum foil, using a rolling pin or bottle, roll each triangle out thinly, and set aside. Combine the butter flavoring, sweetener and egg and beat with a wire whisk or fork. Dip the bread into this egg mixture to absorb all of it, then return it to the aluminum foil and roll each piece up like a crescent roll. Place in a Teflon pan and brown on both sides. Serve with juice, a DW spread and coffee.

SPINACH BREAKFAST SURPRISE

Raw spinach leaves	1 teaspoon chopped parsley
Hard boiled eggs	
Salt and pepper to taste	1 tablespoon lemon juice
Dash garlic powder	⅛ teaspoon imitation butter flavoring

Try these spinach rolls when you want something different for breakfast:

Wash raw spinach leaves and drain well. Boil eggs and mash. Season with salt, pepper, garlic powder and parsley. Place 1 or 2 tablespoons of this mixture on each spinach leaf and roll, using small metal skewers to hold each. Place in a shallow baking dish. Pour lemon juice and butter flavoring over each roll and broil until leaf is softened.

One egg equals a breakfast serving.

LUNCH

CROUTONS
(Lunch only)

1 slice white bread   **Garlic powder (optional)**

Put bread through the toaster twice and cut into small squares. Use as a topping for any lunch soup. For garlic croutons, sprinkle both sides with garlic powder *before* toasting.

CONSOMMÉ WITH CROUTONS
(Lunch only)

1 slice white bread   **1 chicken bouillon cube**
Garlic powder   **dissolved in a cup of**
  Parsley flakes   **hot water**

Toast the bread, sprinkled with garlic powder on both sides, twice. Cut into small cubes. Float these croutons on the hot bouillon soup and garnish with parsley flakes.

SPLIT PEA SOUP WITH CROUTONS
(Lunch only)

1 can asparagus   **Dash paprika**
  (save juice)   **1 slice white bread**
½ can French-style   **(optional)**
  string beans, drained   **Salt and pepper to taste**
½ teaspoon parsley

Put the asparagus and its juice through the blender with the string beans, parsley and seasonings. Heat mixture in a saucepan with the mushrooms and serve. To make croutons: Toast the bread, cut into squares, and float on the soup.

With croutons use this for lunch only. Without croutons you can have it anytime and it's unlimited.

40

BOUILLABAISSE
(Dinner only)

1 ounce leeks, sliced (optional)	½ pound assorted fish (red snapper, cod, flounder, haddock, lobster tail, shrimp, scallops, sea bass or other fish you prefer)
1 ounce onion, diced	
2 cloves garlic, diced	
2 ounces tomatoes, sliced	
1 chicken bouillon cube dissolved in a cup of hot water	1 package French-style string beans, frozen
Dash saffron	Dash salt
½ bay leaf (do not crush)	Dash cayenne
	Parsley

In large covered Teflon pan, saute the leeks, onion and garlic over a small flame. Remove cover and raise flame to brown the onion. Add the tomato, bouillon, saffron and bay leaf and bring to a boil, then lower the flame. Add all the fish, cut into 2 inch pieces, cover and simmer 10 to 15 minutes. Add the string beans, salt and cayenne, remove the bay leaf and simmer 5 minutes more, or until fish is done. Do not cook more than 30 minutes all together. Serve in a small casserole dish, garnished with parsley.

This recipe equals one dinner fish serving and one dinner vegetable.

BRAISED BEEF

4 or 5 pounds boneless chuck beef	1 tablespoon parsley
2 ounces onion, sliced thin	2 cloves garlic, diced fine
2 ounces carrots, thinly sliced	½ teaspoon dried thyme
3 or 4 stalks celery cut into thin crescents	2 bay leaves
	2 whole cloves
¼ teaspoon pepper	1 chicken bouillon cube dissolved in a cup of hot water

Prepare a sheet of heavy duty foil large enough to wrap roast and all ingredients. Lay foil in shallow roasting pan and place the beef in the center. Under broiler brown meat well on each side, then pour off fat. Add the onion, carrots and celery, in individual groups on the foil. Broil 5 minutes to brown the vegetables, then sprinkle meat with pepper, parsley, garlic, thyme, bay leaves and cloves. Pour just 2 ounces of bouillon broth over meat and seal the foil. Roast in 350° oven 1 ½ hours for medium-rare. If you prefer it well done, open foil, slice meat in half, reseal and roast 20 minutes more. To serve, slice diagonally. Top with DW Braised Beef Sauce, if you like.

Six ounces of meat equal one dinner beef serving and the vegetables equal a dinner serving. The Braised Beef Sauce is one glass of milk for the day.

BRAISED BEEF SAUCE DW

⅓ cup dry powdered   Salt
   skim milk   Pepper
   Drippings from a
   roasted beef

Refrigerate roast beef drippings and skim off fat. Reheat. Dissolve the powdered milk in the drippings and put mixture through blender. Add salt and pepper to taste. Heat and serve as a side dish.

This recipe equals one glass of milk.

BRAISED CHICKEN LIVERS

8 ounces chicken livers   ½ teaspoon dried dill
1 can mushrooms (save   1 ounce diced scallions
   liquid)   3 ounces green peas
⅓ cup dry powdered   DW rice (or mashed
   skim milk   cauliflower)

Brown the chicken livers in a Teflon frypan on a small flame, then reduce flame further just to keep warm. Put half the mushrooms and the liquid through blender with the dry powdered milk. Pour mixture over livers in pan. Add the rest of the mushrooms, dried dill, scallions and green peas. Stir together and heat. Serve over a bed of DW rice, or over cooked and mashed cauliflower.

This recipe equals a dinner beef serving, a dinner vegetable and one glass of milk.

CHICKEN LIVERS EN BROCHETTE

8 ounces chicken livers   4 ounces onion, sliced
4 green peppers,   or diced
   quartered   DW Rice
½ pound fresh mushrooms Salt and pepper

On skewers alternate: liver, quartered green peppers and whole mushrooms. Cover broiler pan with aluminum foil. Lay skewers on it and broil 2 inches from flame, 5 to 6 minutes. Turn skewer and broil second side to doneness you like. Serve on a bed of DW rice-and-onions, with a salad of greens.

To make onion-rice: Sauté the onion in covered Teflon pan without water 10 minutes. Remove cover, raise flame to brown. Season DW rice to taste with salt and pepper.

As soon as livers are done, combine onions and DW rice, mixing well. Place on platter. Top with the livers and vegetable.

This meal is a dinner beef serving and a dinner vegetable.

CHICKEN A LA KING

6 ounces cooked, diced chicken	¼ teaspoon (optional) imitation butter flavoring
1 green pepper, chopped	Dash salt
1 pimiento, chopped	Dash pepper
4 ounces onion, diced	½ cup skim milk

In double boiler, cook together the chicken, chopped green pepper, chopped pimiento and onion, for 20 minutes. Add the imitation butter flavoring. To the skim milk add salt and pepper and combine this seasoned milk with the chicken and vegetables. Continue cooking, stirring gently, until slightly thickened (about 10 minutes), and serve.

Entire recipe equals one dinner serving and half a cup of milk.

CHICKEN CASSEROLE

2 ½ pound chicken, cut as for Southern fry	½ teaspoon powdered ginger
1 bay leaf	8 ounces tomato juice
1 clove garlic, minced or ½ teaspoon garlic powder	12 shallots
½ teaspoon salt (optional)	4 carrots cut into strips
8 peppercorns	4 stalks of celery, sliced diagonally

Pat the chicken dry with paper toweling and arrange in 2 ½ quart casserole dish. Add the bay leaf, garlic, salt (if you like), peppercorns, ginger and tomato juice. Cover and bake 1 hour in 350° oven. Remove cover and add the rest of the ingredients. Continue baking uncovered ½ hour more. If vegetables aren't tender, cover and cook 10 minutes longer to soften them.

Half the chicken equals one dinner portion. Four ounces of the carrots and shallots combined equal one dinner vegetable.

LOBSTER BOATS GLACÉ

2 quarts water	2 ounces green scallion tops, minced
¼ cup white vinegar	Green pepper slivers
½ teaspoon salt (optional)	
1 small bay leaf	1 tablespoon lemon juice
1 teaspoon dry terragon	2 fresh or frozen lobster tails (4 ounces each)
1 teaspoon chervil leaves	

In a large covered pot bring two quarts of water to a rapid boil. Add all ingredients but lobster tails. As soon as water is boiling again, add the lobster tails. Reduce flame and let simmer six minutes. Remove lobster to cool. With kitchen shears, cut the soft undershell of the tails and lift out lobster meat, without breaking the shells. Set shells aside. Use a very sharp knife to cut two lengthwise slices from each tail and set these aside. Dice the rest of the lobster meat into ½ inch cubes. Mix with the green pepper and onion from lobster pot and return mixture to the tail shells. Arrange tails in deep dishes with the two long lobster slices placed crosswise like oars on a boat. Pour aspic glaze (see recipe below) over the stuffed shells and chill in the refrigerator. Serve on a bed of crisp lettuce or with a large tossed salad and DW Mayonnaise spread.

This recipe equals one dinner seafood serving plus two ounces of a dinner vegetable.

ASPIC GLACÉ FOR LOBSTER BOATS
(Or any seafood or vegetables—unlimited)

1 envelope unflavored gelatine	1 chicken bouillon cube
1 cup cold water	1 tablespoon lemon juice

Sprinkle the gelatine into a cup of cold water to soften. Add one chicken bouillon cube and heat over a small flame, stirring until gelatine and chicken bouillon are completely dissolved. Add the lemon juice and stir. Pour mixture over seafood (or vegetables) and chill in refrigerator.

PARISIENNE SWEETBREADS
(Cheapest thing in the store)

½ pound lung (buy it whole and have your butcher cube it)	1 pound fresh mushrooms or large can, drained
4 ounces tomato juice	4 ounces onion
4 ounces water	1 box frozen cauliflower
	1 can French-style string beans, drained

In a covered saucepan simmer the cubed lung, tomato juice, water, mushrooms, onion and cauliflower for 2 hours, then add the string beans. Continue cooking, covered, on a small flame for another 30 minutes. Serve the meat and other vegetables on a nest of the cauliflower.

This recipe equals one dinner meat serving, one dinner vegetable and four ounces of tomato juice for the day.

QUENELLES WITH BROILED SHALLOTS

10 ounces pike (including
    skin and bones)
½ green pepper, diced
1 stalk celery, diced
    Dash garlic powder
½ teaspoon terragon
    vinegar
1 tablespoon water

½ cup tomato juice
⅓ cup powdered dry skim
    milk
½ teaspoon parsley flakes
    Dash paprika
    Dash pepper
4 ounces whole shallots

Have your fish dealer fillet the pike. At home, chop the fish with the diced green pepper, celery, garlic powder, vinegar, water and one ounce of the tomato juice. Set aside. In a medium sized bowl, mix the powdered milk with the parsley flakes and paprika. Line your broiler with aluminum foil and moisten the top with a few drops of tomato juice. Moisten your hands with cold water and shape the fish mixture into small oval dumplings, then dip each dumpling into the bowl of seasoned milk powder and place it on the moistened foil. Broil about 2 inches from the flame. Brown on one side, turn carefully, pour rest of tomato juice over all and brown the second side. Serve with asparagus spears, lemon wedges and broiled shallots.

For broiled shallots: Steam shallots in 1/8 cup water just until tender to a fork test, then broil with the quenelles.

This recipe equals one dinner fish serving and one dinner vegetable.

"SAUSAGES" REMOULADE

½ pound frankfurter
    "Specials"

Basic Remoulade
Sauce # 1

Cut the "Specials" (or any frankfurters) lengthwise in half, and open them flat. Broil on rack, skin side up, until brown (about 10 minutes). Turn and brown other side 10 minutes. Top with Basic Remoulade Sauce # 1.

This equals one dinner beef serving and a dinner vegetable. Serve with French fried cauliflowerettes (see index), which you can brown on the broiler along with the specials.

SHRIMP CASSEROLE FRANCAISE

6 ounces cooked shrimp
for dinner, 3 ounces
for lunch
1 tablespoon mustard
powder
1 head cauliflower,
overcooked
1 can cut asparagus,
drained (or 1 package,
frozen, cooked
and drained)

1 can sliced mushrooms,
drained (reserve
the liquid)
⅛ teaspoon paprika
2 or 3 sprigs parsley
⅓ cup dry skim milk
powder

Sprinkle mustard lightly through the shrimp. Drain the overcooked cauliflower and mash fine. Line the bottom of a casserole dish with half of the cauliflower. Place a layer of shrimp, asparagus and mushrooms on it. Cover with a layer of the remaining cauliflower and top with the powdered skim milk. Decorate the top with paprika and parsley and pour the mushroom liquid over all. Bake in 350° oven for 30 minutes, or until the top browns.

The dish equals one dinner fish serving plus one glass of milk for the day. Three ounces of shrimp is a lunch serving.

SHRIMP PEPPER BOATS
WITH REMOULADE SAUCE

6 ounces cooked shrimp
2 ounces chives, chopped
fine
Remoulade Sauce #2
2 green peppers

Lettuce
Radish roses
Imitation butter flavor-
ing (only if you
serve hot)

After cooking shrimp reserve a few and chop up the rest. Mix chopped shrimp with the chives and toss mixture with Remoulade Sauce #2. Set aside. Halve the green peppers lengthwise and remove seeds. Fill pepper boats with the shrimp mixture, garnishing with the whole shrimp. Serve the boats on a bed of lettuce and with a few radish roses.

This recipe equals one dinner seafood serving and two ounces of a dinner vegetable.

TO SERVE HOT: Use the same recipe but make aluminum cups to hold each pepper boat and moisten the outside of each pepper lightly with butter flavoring before setting it into the cup. Place the cups in a baking dish and bake for 10 minutes, until peppers become tender. Serve hot with a

side dish of asparagus spears and with tossed green salad.
This recipe equals one fish dinner and a dinner vegetable.

STUFFED CUCUMBER BOATS REMOULADE

6 ounces codfish, cooked and flaked	1 cup Remoulade Sauce #2
3 cucumbers	Lettuce
1 tablespoon lemon juice	Parsley
2 ounces onion, diced	Paprika

Broil codfish without seasoning near the flame for 5 minutes on each side (or until tender). With a fork, make into flakes and set aside. Carefully halve the cucumbers lengthwise and scoop out the centers gently, just a bit deeper than the seeds. Combine the pulp with the fish, lemon juice, onion and 1 cup of Remoulade Sauce #2. Refill cucumber boats with the mixture. Serve on crisp lettuce and sprinkle the top lightly with parsley and paprika.

This recipe is one dinner seafood serving and four ounces of a dinner vegetable.

VEAL BLANQUETTE

2 pounds veal, cubed	1 chicken bouillon cube dissolved in 1 cup hot water
Salt	
Pepper	
1 clove garlic, minced fine	3 carrots
2 ounces onion, diced fine	2 leeks
2 tablespoons fresh dill, chopped	1 cup buttermilk
½ teaspoon nutmeg	1 cauliflower

Sprinkle veal cubes with salt and pepper, then brown well in Teflon pan. Transfer to a casserole dish and add the garlic, onion, half the dill, and the nutmeg and chicken bouillon. Cover and bake in preheated 350° oven 1 hour. While casserole is cooking: Split leeks in half and rinse them, cut the carrots into thin strips and add these to the casserole (stir and add water if needed). Also, overcook the cauliflower, drain well, mash it fine or put it through a potato ricer, and transfer it to a serving platter. When the meat in the casserole is tender, add the buttermilk, mixing well, to make a cream sauce. As soon as the sauce is hot, spoon it over the cauliflower. Top with the veal and vegetables and garnish with the remaining dill.

Six ounces of veal equal a dinner meat serving. Four ounces of carrots and leeks are a dinner vegetable. The sauce equals one cup of milk.

SOUPS, SIDE DISHES, SNACKS AND SAUCES

BROCCOLI SOUP
(Unlimited)

2 chicken bouillon
cubes
2 cups hot water

2 packages frozen
chopped broccoli
Some chopped pimiento

Dissolve bouillon cubes in hot water and set aside. Cook both packages of chopped broccoli in 1 cup of the bouillon until done. Let cool and put the mixture through the blender until completely pulverized. Return mixture to saucepan and reheat in the second cup of bouillon, just bringing it to a boil. This looks lovely garnished with a small amount of chopped pimiento for color, and it also tastes fabulous!

CREAM OF CAULIFLOWER SOUP

1 medium cauliflower
2 chicken bouillon cubes

2 cups hot water
Dash parsley flakes

Wash and break cauliflower into flowerettes and set aside. Dissolve the bouillon cubes in hot water. Cook the flowerettes in one cup of the bouillon until soft but not mushy. Let cool, then put flowerettes and cooking liquid through the blender for 1 ½ minutes. Return to saucepan and add the second cup of bouillon. Heat just to the boiling point. Serve hot, garnished with parsley flakes.

FRENCH ONION SOUP
(Dinner only)

4 ounces onion, diced
1 can bean sprouts

1 chicken bouillon cube
dissolved in 1 cup boil-
ing water

Saute the onion in a covered Teflon pan 10 minutes or until tender. Drain the bean sprouts bone dry and add to the pan, then raise flame to brown onion and bean sprouts together, until well browned. Add the chicken bouillon and serve hot.

This recipe equals one dinner vegetable.

GREEN PEA SOUP

1 chicken bouillon cube
1 cup hot water

1 box frozen peas,
or 1 can
⅛ teaspoon chervil leaves

Dissolve bouillon cube in the hot water. If frozen peas are used, cook according to box directions. Reserve one teaspoon of peas. Put the rest through the blender with the bouillon. Pour into saucepan, bring to a boil, remove from heat and for a garnish add the teaspoon of whole peas and the chervil leaves.

This recipe equals one dinner vegetable.

VICHYSSOISE
(Dinner only)

1 chicken bouillon cube	1 cup warm skim milk
1 cup hot water	1 teaspoon parsley,
1 box frozen cauliflower	chopped fine
2 ounces onion,	2 ounces chives, chopped
chopped fine	fine

Dissolve bouillon cube in the hot water and place in saucepan with the frozen cauliflower. Simmer for 15 minutes, then let cool. In covered Teflon pan, sauté the chopped onion 5 minutes or until tender, then remove cover and brown onion just- slightly. Put the cauliflower, bouillon and the warm skim milk through the blender for 2 minutes to puree. Add the browned onions and the parsley, and refrigerate. When ready to serve, garnish with the chives.

This recipe equals one dinner vegetable and one cup of milk.

BRAISED CELERY

1 bunch celery	1 chicken bouillon cube,
½ teaspoon salt	dissolved in a cup of
2 ounces onion, minced	hot water
2 ounces canned carrots	

Clean the celery, cutting off the celery root and leaves, but do not separate the stalks. Cut off 5 inches from the bottom for braising (reserve the rest for salads). In a large saucepan bring enough water to cover the celery to a boil. Add salt. Cook celery in the boiling water 10 minutes. Drain, cool, arrange celery in a Teflon frypan and set aside. Chop the onion and canned carrots together. Add the chicken bouillon and pour this braising mix into the frypan. Cover and cook over a small flame until celery is tender to a fork test.

This recipe equals one dinner vegetable.

FRENCH FRIED ONIONS

Onions—up to two
pounds

Slice onions and place the slices in a Teflon frypan. Cook, covered but without water until tender (about 10 minutes). Remove cover, raise flame and stir as the slices brown. Voila—French fried onions! Make two pounds of this at a time. It will keep in your refrigerator, in a covered plastic container, for as long as a week.

Four ounces equal one dinner vegetable.

HORS D'OEUVRE SIDE DISH OR STARTER

8 ounces asparagus spears, or 1 small can
2 ounces cherry tomatoes
1 cucumber, sliced thin (leave skin on)
2 ounces carrots, sliced thin and cooked
1 cup raw cauliflowerettes
½ cup terragon vinegar
⅓ cup water
1 ½ teaspoons liquid non-sugar sweetener
¾ teaspoon salt (optional)
¼ teaspoon pepper
1 teaspoon dried basil

Arrange the five vegetables in rows in a shallow rectangular serving dish. Combine the last six ingredients to make the sauce and pour this over the vegetables. Cover with Saran wrap and refrigerate overnight. Great to make the night before a party.

This recipe equals one dinner vegetable.

MUSHROOM HORS D'OEUVRE
(Unlimited)

Whole small fresh mushrooms, or caps only of large mushrooms
⅓ cup white vinegar
½ teaspoon garlic powder
1 bay leaf
½ teaspoon dehydrated dill, or 3 or 4 sprigs
Dash pepper

In covered Teflon saucepan, using no water, steam mushrooms over a low flame until they are tender (about 10 minutes). Mushrooms will release their own liquid. Add vinegar, garlic powder, all other seasonings. Chill in refrigerator, allowing mushrooms to marinate at least four hours. Strain and serve with picks.

BASIC REMOULADE SAUCE #1

1 tablespoon mild mustard
⅛ teaspoon imitation butter flavoring
Salt and pepper to taste
2 ounces shallots, chopped fine

Combine the mild mustard gradually with the butter flavoring, stirring until you get a smooth consistency. Season to taste with salt and pepper, then stir in the chopped shallots. Try it on cold seafood and meat dinners.

This recipe equals one dinner vegetable.

REMOULADE SAUCE #2

2 tablespoons mild mustard	Salt and pepper to taste
⅛ teaspoon imitation butter flavoring	2 ounces shallots, chopped fine

Combine the mustard and butter flavoring, stirring until you get a smooth consistency. Season to taste with salt and pepper. Stir in the chopped shallots.

This equals two ounces of a dinner vegetable.

SAUCE VINAIGRETTE
(Unlimited)

¼ cup vinegar	1 clove garlic, diced
⅛ teaspoon paprika	2 tablespoons water
½ teaspoon dill, tarragon, rosemary and thyme, mixed	¼ teaspoon liquid non-sugar sweetener

Combine all ingredients in a tightly closed bottle. Store in refrigerator. The flavor improves with age. Shake well and use on any cold salad—it's unlimited!

A TOUCH OF JEWISH

BREAKFAST

CHOPPED VEGETARIAN LIVER
(Breakfast only)

1 hard boiled egg,
mashed with fork
while hot
1 can French-style string
beans
1 can mushrooms, diced
fine

Salt and pepper to
taste
Imitation butter
flavoring
1 slice toast

Mix the mashed egg, string beans, mushrooms, salt and pepper. Add a dash of the butter flavoring. Serve on toast.

DINNERS

BAKED CARP

1 carp
Paprika
Parsley
Garlic powder
5 stalks celery (with
leaves), cut in chunks
3 stalks Chinese caabbage
(with leaves), cut up
1 whole raw cauliflower,
broken into flowerettes
1 pound fresh
mushrooms

3 red peppers, in strips
3 green peppers, in strips
1 can French-style string
beans, drained well
(reserve liquid)
1 can bean sprouts,
drained well
2 large tomatoes, sliced
1 can peas and carrots,
drained well (reserve
liquid)

Have the fish dealer remove the head, fins, tail and scales and cut the carp into 10-ounce portions. Sprinkle fish outside and inside with paprika, parsley, garlic powder. In a long baking pan make a bed of the celery. Top with a layer of Chinese cabbage and continue to build up layers of: cauliflowerettes, mushrooms (break stems from caps), red and green peppers, string beans, bean sprouts. Keep one end of the roasting pan clear and in that end place the onions, topped with the tomatoes. Cover these with the peas and carrots and sprinkle paprika, garlic powder and parsley over them. Lay the carp over all. Bake in 350° oven 15 minutes. Use liquid from string beans if needed while baking, turn fish and bake another 15 minutes. Fish should be crisp.

Each portion of fish equals a dinner fish serving and four ounces of the mixed vegetables in the end-section are one dinner vegetable. The other vegetables are unlimited.

BAKED SHAD

1 shad
Paprika
Garlic powder
1 large onion, sliced
1 can green peas and
carrots with liquid

1 can green beans,
drained
2 stalks celery

Have fish dealer scale and clean the shad and cut it into 10 ounce portions. Sprinkle all over (inside, too) with paprika and garlic powder. Place onion slices in shallow baking pan. Add green peas and carrots, including the liquid and the green beans and celery. Top with the shad. Bake in 350° oven 15 minutes, turn carefully and bake another 15 minutes or until fish is brown.

A ten ounce portion is one dinner fish serving and 4 ounces of mixed vegetables equal one dinner vegetable.

BOILED CARP

10 ounces carp
1 stalk celery, diced
2 ounces carrot, diced
2 ounces onion, diced
Salt

Pepper
White horseradish
Lettuce
Cucumber

Ask the fish dealer to scale the carp. At home put it in a saucepan with the celery, carrot and onion. Add dashes of salt, pepper, and water just to cover, and bring to a boil. Reduce flame and simmer, covered, ½ hour until carrots are tender. Serve fish soup hot or cold. If you refrigerate it 2 or 3 hours, the soup will jell and it's marvelous served on a crisp lettuce and cucumber salad, with white horseradish on the side.

This recipe is one dinner fish serving and one dinner vegetable.

CHICKEN DUMPLINGS

1 pullet (4 ½ pounds)	1 small onion
2 stalks celery, sliced	½ green pepper, diced
½ bay leaf	½ red pepper, diced
1 sliced carrot	Salt and pepper to taste
2 cups water	1 egg white

Skin and bone the raw chicken. Discard skin. Simmer the bones, bay leaf and carrots in the water at least ½ hour. Meanwhile chop the raw chicken meat, onion and diced peppers together in a chopping bowl. Season with salt and pepper. Fold in the egg white and continue chopping until fluffy. Wet hands with cold water, then form mixture into small balls (1 or 2 inches). Raise flame to bring the simmering broth to a boil and gently place dumplings in it. Lower heat, cover, cook ¾ hour more. Delicious hot or cold!

To serve hot: Remove dumplings and chill broth. Skim off fat, return dumplings and reheat.

To serve cold: Pour de-fatted broth over dumplings and refrigerate to jell.

Six ounces equal one dinner serving and a dinner vegetable.

CHOPPED CHICKEN LIVER

4 ounces onion, diced fine	Sliced cucumber
8 ounces chicken livers	Celery
Lettuce	

Sauté the onion in a covered Teflon pan, then remove cover to brown. Add the chicken livers, browning about 5 minutes, just until done. With fork, mash chicken livers and mix well with the browned onion. Serve hot or chilled over a large bed of crisp lettuce. Garnish with sliced cucumber and celery stalks.

This recipe equals one dinner beef serving and a dinner vegetable.

FLANKEN (BOILED BEEF)

6 glasses water	Bunch parsley
2 pounds lean flanken	Fresh dill
1 pound fresh mushrooms	
1 package frozen French-style string beans (thawed)	

Have butcher trim all fat from flanken. Place in a saucepan with the water and bring to boil. Skim off matter that will rise, until the top is generally clear. Add the mushrooms, thawed string beans. Wash and tie together with white thread the parsley and fresh dill, and add them to saucepan. Cover and simmer until meat is tender (about 1 ½ hours). To serve: Remove bone, refrigerate the soup, skim off all fat, and add any unlimited vegetables you like. Reheat and enjoy!

Six ounces of meat equals a dinner beef serving.

"CHULANT" TZIMMES AND FLANKEN

**6 ounces cooked flanken
DW style**

**4 ounces carrot and
butternut tzimmes**

Cube the cooked flanken. Mix 6 ounces with 4 ounces of the 'tzimmes." Place in Teflon frypan, cover and then place frypan on a potato baker. On top of the stove, heat thoroughly on very low flame.

Six ounces of "Chulant" equals one dinner beef serving and a dinner vegetable.

SWEET "CHULANT"

**6 ounces cooked flanken
4 ounces carrot and
butternut tzimmes**

**2 capfuls No-Cal cherry
syrup**

Cube the cooked flanken. Combine 6 ounces with 4 ounces tzimmes. Add the cherry syrup. Place in Teflon frypan, cover and place frypan on a potato baker. On top of stove, heat thoroughly on very low flame.

Six ounces is a dinner beef serving and a dinner vegetable.

JEWISH MOTHER'S BOILED CHICKEN AND SOUP

**4-pound chicken,
quartered
8 glasses water
Salt and pepper to taste
5 or 6 stalks celery
Large bunch parsley
and dill**

**1 large parsnip
4 ounces tomato juice
Dash paprika
Garlic powder
Parsley flakes**

Clean the chicken and place it in a large pot with the water. Season with salt and pepper. Bring to a boil, and skim off the top so the broth is clear. Add the celery, parsley and dill (washed and tied together with white thread), and the parsnip. Cover and simmer 1 to 1 ½ hours, until breast of chicken is tender to a fork test. Remove chicken, greens and celery. Refrigerate the soup. When fat congeals, skim it off, discard and set the de-fatted broth aside. Remove skin from chicken meat. Place on broiler and pour tomato juice or de-fatted broth over it. Sprinkle with paprika, garlic powder, parsley flakes. Broil close to flame to brown quickly. Serve with white horseradish sauce on the side.

The chicken broth, de-fatted, is an anytime food. A quarter of the chicken equals one dinner serving.

GEFILTE FISH

3 ½ pounds pike and white
fish (or carp), ground
together
2 eggs
1 small onion, diced fine
2 drops liquid non-sugar
sweetener

Salt and pepper, to
taste
2 ½ cups water
2 carrots, sliced
diagonally
2 to 3 celery stalks,
diced

Have your fish dealer grind the fish and pack the head, bones and other scraps separately to take with you. Place the ground fish, eggs, onion, sweetener, salt and pepper in a large chopping bowl and chop all very fine, gradually adding ½ cup of water. When mixture is light and fluffy, moisten both hands with cold water and shape fish into balls about 2 inches in diameter. Set aside. Make a sauce by placing the fish scraps on the bottom of a saucepan, covering them with the carrots and celery, and adding two cups of water. Bring rapidly to a boil, lower flame and cook ¾ hour covered, until carrots and celery are tender. Remove cover, raise flame and as the water boils up, gently lower the fish balls onto the bed of vegetables. Cover and simmer 2 hours. If water boils out, add more so that you have a gravy to serve at the end. This can be served hot or cold. It's a wonderful Passover recipe, a great dish any time of the year!

Six ounces equals one dinner fish serving and three ounces is a lunch portion.

KNOBLE-BORSCHT WITH FLANKEN

1 large can sliced beets
(or 1 package fresh)
1 ½ cups water
2 to 3 teaspoons lemon
juice
Dash salt
Dash pepper

2 teaspoons liquid non-
sugar sweetener
1 clove garlic or ½ teaspoon garlic powder
1 small onion
1 pound flanken

Trim all fat from flanken. Place all ingredients (flanken too) in a large pot and bring to boil. Lower flame and simmer, covered, 1 to 1 ½ hours or until meat is tender. Remove flanken. Slice. Serve with boiled cabbage or mashed cauliflower.

Six ounces of sliced flanken equals a dinner beef serving. A small bowl of Knoble-Borscht equals a dinner vegetable.

KOSHER STYLE STUFFED SAUSAGE

Fat frankfurter "Special" (8 ounces)	1 small can mushrooms, drained and chopped
½ cup canned crushed pineapple (unsweetened)	1 green pepper, diced fine
	4 ounces green peas

Cut "Special" frank lengthwise but only partially through. Open wide as you would a frankfurter roll and set aside. Mix the pineapple, mushrooms and green pepper. Fill "Special" with the mixture and use small skewers to hold it together. Broil until "Special" is well done—delicious served with 4 ounces of green peas.

This recipe equals one dinner beef serving, a dinner vegetable and one fruit.

STUFFED BREAST OF VEAL—JEWISH STYLE

Breast of veal, 5 pounds	Parsley
Paprika	DW Mushroom Sprouts
Garlic powder	stuffing
Pepper	1 chicken bouillon cube
Salt	1 cup hot water

Have butcher cut pocket in a 5 pound breast of veal. Before stuffing, rub veal with paprika, garlic powder, pepper, salt and parsley. Fill pocket with Mushroom-Sprouts stuffing and close pocket with skewers. Place in baking dish, stuffing side up. Dissolve chicken bouillon cube in the hot water and pour over veal in baking dish. Roast in 350° oven two hours, turning once. Add bouillon if liquid cooks out.

Ten ounces cooked is a dinner meat serving and the stuffing equals one ounce of a dinner vegetable.

MUSHROOM-SPROUTS STUFFING
(For five pound veal)

2 ¼ pounds fresh mushrooms, or 2 cans (8 ounces each)	Dash cayenne powder
1 can bean sprouts, drained	Salt (optional)
	¼ cup tomato juice
3 ounces onion, diced	Dash parsley
3 green peppers, diced	Dash paprika

Chop drained mushrooms or boil fresh ones in water until tender, then drain and chop. Add bean sprouts, the diced onion, diced green pepper, cayenne powder and salt to taste, mixing well. In a Teflon pan sauté everything in the tomato juice until pepper is soft. Let cool, add the parsley and paprika—a perfect stuffing for veal!

Even if you eat *all* the stuffing, it's just three ounces of a dinner vegetable and ¼ cup of tomato juice. Serve with one ounce of sliced tomatoes to complete your dinner vegetable for the day.

But why not share the stuffing? If you eat only half, you can have 2 ½ ounces of another dinner vegetable. If you eat a quarter of it, you can have three ounces of another vegetable.

SOUPS, SIDE DISHES, SNACKS AND SAUCES

JEWISH KNOBLE-BORSCHT
(Garlic-beet soup)

1 **large can sliced beets (or 1 package fresh)**	2 **teaspoons liquid non-sugar sweetener**
1 ½ **cups water**	1 **clove garlic (or ½ teaspoon garlic powder)**
2 **or 3 teaspoons lemon juice**	1 **small onion**
Dash salt	**Shredded cabbage (optional)**
Dash pepper	
Giblets of 1 chicken	

In a saucepan cook all ingredients together until the giblets are tender (about 30 minutes). Test for the winey taste you prefer and adjust by adding sweetener or lemon juice. Knoble (pronounced with a hard "K") means "garlic". This garlic borscht is delicious hot with shredded cabbage, cooked separately, drained and added.

A small bowl equals a dinner vegetable.

JEWISH MOTHER'S VEGETABLE SOUP (ALMOST)
(Anytime soup)

⅓ **package French-style string beans, frozen**	1 **cup tomato juice**
3 **or 4 leaves cabbage, shredded**	½ **quart water**
	2 **chicken bouillon cubes**
3 **stalks celery, diced**	½ **bay leaf, crushed**
1 **or 2 green peppers, diced**	**Salt and pepper to taste**

Cook all ingredients in a saucepan 20 to 25 minutes, until vegetables are tender. Strain the liquid into a jar. Put the vegetables through the blender with a few tablespoons of the liquid. When blended, add the mixture to the jar and mix well. You can add 1 can of drained mushrooms or bean sprouts, if you like. Heat to serve. Have a bowl now and refrigerate the rest.

One bowl equals only two ounces of tomato juice.

SPLIT PEA SOUP WITH NOODLES
(Unlimited)

1 can asparagus (save the juice)	Dash paprika
	Salt and pepper to taste
½ can French-style string beans, drained	½ can bean sprouts, drained
½ teaspoon parsley	½ can mushrooms, drained

Put first 5 ingredients and the asparagus juice through the blender. Then add the bean sprouts and mushrooms, heat and serve.

CARROT AND BUTTERNUT TZIMMES

1 bunch carrots	1 bottle diet cherry soda
1 butternut squash	Dash cinnamon

Peel and slice the carrots and place in Teflon frypan. Peel squash, halve it, remove seeds, cut it into large chunks and add it to frypan. Add the soda and cinnamon. Cook, covered, on medium flame until carrots are soft (most of soda will have cooked out). Marvelous with roast chicken or with flanken.

Four ounces is a dinner vegetable.

HOLIDAY KUGEL
(Anytime food)

1 pound summer squash	½ cup dry milk powder
1 medium sized pineapple	1 tablespoon cinnamon
¼ cup No-Cal cherry syrup	2 drops vanilla extract

Wash the squash well and slice it. Peel and slice the pineapple. Place the slices in saucepan with the syrup and simmer, covered, until tender (do not add any water). Let cool and put everything through blender. In a small bowl combine the powdered milk, cinnamon and vanilla. Dust the bottom of a small (4 to 5 inch diameter) aluminum pie dish with half of the dry mixture. Pour in 1 cupful of the squash-pineapple mix. Top with the remaining powdered milk. Bake in 350° oven until bone dry (1 to 2 hours). Serve hot

or cold. Great as a side dish, with coffee or tea.
One kugel equals a fruit and a glass of milk.

JEWISH EGGPLANT STEAK

2 **large eggplants**	½ **teaspoon oregano**
Dash parsley	2 **tablespoons tomato juice**
Dash paprika	**Salt and pepper, to**
Dash garlic powder	**taste**

Slice two large eggplants lengthwise into steaks ¾ inch thick. Do not peel. Cover steaks liberally on both sides with the parsley, paprika, garlic and oregano. If you are lazy (as I am) spread out heavy gauge aluminum foil to make a "tray" and moisten it with the tomato juice. Arrange eggplant slices on foil. Broil in middle portion of broiler—usually the second rack position—until tops are crusted like charcoal broiled steaks. Turn. Season the uncooked side with salt and pepper over the tomato juice bits that will cling to them. Broil until browned and tender (about 10 minutes). These are fabulous, but don't brown them too fast or they won't be thoroughly cooked.

Four ounces of eggplant steak equals one dinner vegetable. *It's so tempting, be sure to weigh your portion!*

JEWISH SCHAV WITH SOUR CREAM

1 **pound sorrel leaves (also**	**Salt to taste**
called sour grass, schav)	8 **jars**
8 **glasses cold water**	½ **glass buttermilk**

Remove leaves from stems and wash well under cold running water to remove all sand. Drain. Taking a handful of leaves at a time, shred with very sharp knife. Place in large pot. Wash stems thoroughly and discard the scrawny ones. Tie the thick stems (they have the flavor) together with white sewing thread, winding thread around lightly several times. Place on top of sorrel leaves in pot. Add the water and salt and bring to a boil. Reduce heat and simmer 5 minutes. Taste and add salt if desired. Discard tied stems. Let schav cool. Pour into jars and refrigerate. To drink: Shake, pour into glass, add ½ glass buttermilk and stir.

This is an anytime drink that equals one-half glass of milk.

JEWISH SPRING SALAD
(Anytime)

¼ **head lettuce, cut into**	2 **or 3 radishes, diced**
bite size pieces	1 **cup buttermilk**
½ **cucumber, diced**	**Salt and pepper, to**
1 **green pepper, diced**	**taste**

Mix everything together in a salad bowl. Add salt and pepper and toss. An anytime salad snack.

This recipe equals one glass of milk.

STEWED PINEAPPLE COMPOTE
(Anytime)

1 **pound summer squash**	¼ **cup No-Cal cherry**
1 **medium sized pineapple**	**syrup (or any flavor)**

Wash the squash well and slice it. Peel and slice the pineapple. Place slices in a saucepan with the syrup and simmer, covered, until tender (do not add water). Remove from flame and cool. Put everything through blender. Refrigerate and serve cold for dessert.

One cup equals one fruit for the day.

DILL DRESSING

⅓ **cup vinegar**	**Fresh dill**
3 **quarter-grain saccharine tablets (water soluble)**	

Snip dill into small pieces with kitchen shears. Dissolve saccharine in the vinegar, then add dill. Chill in refrigerator. Shake well before serving. Delicious over greens and especially good with sliced cucumber.

SOUR CREAM-HORSERADISH DRESSING
(A quickie)

1 **cup buttermilk**	1 **teaspoon lemon juice**
1 **tablespoon white horseradish**	**Dash salt**
1 **teaspoon prepared mustard**	**Dash pepper**

Combine everything, mixing until smooth. Try this over a serving of flaked tuna and a large bed of crisp lettuce.

This recipe equals one glass of milk.

SIDE TRIPS—England, Ireland, Holland, Belgium, Germany, Spain, Hungary, Poland, Rumania, Sicily, Greece

ENGLISH **CINNAMON TOAST**
(Breakfast or lunch only

1 slice white bread   **Dash cinnamon**
  enriched

Just sprinkle the bread lightly with cinnamon on both sides and toast. It's delicious plain, or with DW orange marmalade.

ENGLISH   **DW ORANGE MARMALADE**

1 orange   **3 tablespoons non-sugar**
4 ounces unsweetened   **liquid sweetener**
  orange juice, fresh or   **1 package unflavored**
  frozen   **gelatine**
  Dash salt

Wash the whole orange well and grate off the skin with a grater. Mix the grated rind into the orange juice. Add the salt and liquid sweetener. Segment the peeled orange into small sections, removing any skin and seeds, and set aside. Empty gelatine into a large saucepan. Add the orange juice and stir. Bring to a boil to dissolve gelatine. Shut flame and add orange sections. Refrigerate. You should have one cup of orange marmalade.

This equals two fruits for the day. Use half (one fruit) for breakfast, the rest another time.

ENGLISH **MUSTARD BROILED MACKEREL**
(Lunch or Dinner)

1 whole mackerel   **Garlic powder**
  Paprika   **Prepared mustard**
  Parsley

Have fish dealer cut off the head, tail, fins, and scale the fish, and weigh it again (it should weigh about 10 ounces). Sprinkle with paprika, parsley, garlic powder, then coat the

62

skin and the belly (inside) with mustard. Broil close to the flame until crisp and well browned on one side. Turn and brown other side. Easy and delicious!

This is a dinner fish serving. Four ounces is a lunch serving.

For dinner, try it with a mixture of carrots and peas, and French-style string beans, bean sprouts, mushrooms and shredded Chinese cabbage. Heat, drain and season with white pepper and garlic powder. Four ounces of carrots and peas are one dinner vegetable.

ENGLISH   **ENGLISH KIDNEY PIE**

1 **pound veal kidney**	2 **heads cauliflower,**
1 **bouillon cube dissolved**	**broken into very small**
in 1 cup hot water	**cauliflowerettes**
½ **cup water**	1 **pound whole button**
1 **tablespoon tomato juice**	**mushrooms**
⅛ **teaspoon pepper**	**Dry skim milk powder**
4 **ounces carrots, slivered**	
4 **ounces white onion,**	
diced	

Cut the veal kidney into cubes and brown these in a Teflon pan for 10 minutes, over high flame. Add the chicken bouillon, ½ cup water, the tomato juice, pepper, carrots, onions and 6 ounces of cauliflowerettes (reserve the rest). Cover pan and simmer 1 ½ hours. For the last 10 minutes, add the mushrooms. Transfer to two serving casserole dishes to make separate portions. To make a top crust for each: Overcook the rest of the cauliflower, drain well, mash fine and spread across the top of the casserole dishes. Sprinkle 1/3 cup of dry powdered milk on each casserole. Brown under the broiler.

Each casserole is a dinner meat serving. Four ounces of sauce and vegetables are a dinner vegetable and one glass of milk. (If you omit the powdered milk, you can enjoy the milk separately as a snack the same day.)

ENGLISH   **OYSTERS ROYALE**

1 **can chopped spinach,**	8 **ounces oysters**
drained	**Parsley**
½ **glass buttermilk**	2 **or 3 drops soy sauce**
4 **ounces onion, sliced**	1 **capful lemon juice**

Fill a small baking dish halfway to the top with creamed spinach* and top this with the oysters. Cover them liberally with parsley flakes. Add the soy sauce and lemon juice and cover the baking dish with aluminum foil. In preheated 350° oven bake 15 minutes, then remove foil so oysters brown. You can also make this under the broiler, using the foil cover to prevent burning.

*TO MAKE CREAMED SPINACH: Heat 1 can chopped spinach and drain well. Add ½ glass buttermilk and 4 ounces sliced onion. Mix thoroughly.

This is a dinner seafood serving, a dinner vegetable and ½ glass of milk.

ENGLISH ANYTIME WATERCRESS SOUP
(Unlimited)

1 **bunch watercress**	**Green pepper, diced**
3 **or 4 cups chicken bouillon or fat-free broth**	**Parsley**

Wash the watercress well to remove sand and discard coarse stems. Put the watercress and one cup of bouillon through the blender until fine but not pureed. Add this mixture to the rest of broth and simmer 5 minutes in a saucepan. Garnish with diced green pepper and parsley.

IRISH FINNAN HADDIE

8 **ounces finnan haddie**	**Dash pepper**
Lettuce	**Oregano**
1 **can mushrooms, drained**	**Garlic powder**
1 **can bean sprouts, drained**	**Paprika**
1 **green pepper, in strips**	⅛ **cup tomato juice**
Parsley flakes	4 **ounces French fried onions** (see index)

Try a "licking test" on the raw fish for saltiness. If very salty, soak fish in milk to cover, 1 hour on each side, then discard the milk. Broil 5 minutes on each side. Serve on a bed of lettuce.

Try this delicious side dish of DW vegetables: Place mushrooms, bean sprouts, green pepper and the seasonings in 1/8 cup of tomato juice and bring to a boil in Teflon pan. Reduce flame, cover and simmer until pepper is tender to fork test. Drain and combine with 4 ounces of French fried onions.

The finnan haddie is a dinner fish serving and the side dish is a dinner vegetable.

IRISH BOILED BEEF

4 pounds brisket of beef
Boiling water
½ cup carrots, diced
2 onions, sliced
2 stalks celery

3 or 4 sprigs parsleyy
1 bay leaf
Dash salt
Pepper
1 box frozen cauliflower

Place the brisket of beef in a deep saucepan and add boiling water just to cover. Add the carrots and simmer ½ hour. Add the onions, celery, parsley, bayleaf and a dash of salt and pepper. Simmer 2 ½ hours, or until meat is tender to a fork test. Cool, refrigerate and skim off fat. Carve beef diagonally and reheat in its sauce. Overcook the cauliflower, then drain and mash. Use as a nest for the beef on the serving platter.

For variation you can cook the beef in DW brown sauce rather than the boiling water (See index).

Six ounces of meat is a dinner beef serving and ½ cup of vegetables and sauce are a dinner vegetable.

IRISH STEW

Shoulder of lamb,
trimmed well
4 ounces carrots, sliced
4 ounces small onions
2 or 3 stalks celery (with leaves)

2 or 3 stalks Chinese
cabbage (with leaves)
Pinch thyme
Dash salt
Pepper

Have the butcher remove the lamb bone and cut meat into cubes. At home trim any fat. In a deep saucepan make a layer of meat and top it with a layer of sliced vegetables. Add seasonings, and water just to cover the meat. Simmer 2 ½ hours in covered pot. If the water cooks out, add small amounts at a time, as needed. Let cool, refrigerate and skim off fat. Reheat to serve. This is a good make-ahead meal.

Six ounces of lamb equals a dinner beef serving and ½ cup of the carrots and onion sauce is a dinner vegetable.

STUFFED CUCUMBER DRUMS

6 ounces cooked beef or
lamb
3 large cucumbers
1 bouillon cube dissolved
in 1 cup hot water
2 tablespoons tomato juice
2 ounces onion, chopped
fine

1 teaspoon parsley
Dash pepper
Oregano
Garlic powder
⅛ teaspoon imitation
butter flavoring

Cut the cucumbers into 3 inch chunks and peel a center strip of skin from each chunk. Scoop out the centers carefully. In a 4-quart saucepan, bring to a boil just enough water to cover the cucumbers, and then boil them 5 minutes. Drain well and set aside to cool. Meantime, chop the cucumber centers together with the cooked beef or lamb. Combine this mix with ¼ cup of the bouillon, the tomato juice, onion, parsley and dashes of pepper, oregano and garlic powder. Mix thoroughly. Fill the cucumber chunks with the mixture. Coat a pyrex dish with the butter flavoring and arrange cucumbers in it. Cover or seal with foil and bake in 350° oven 15 minutes. Uncover for the last 5 minutes. If bouillon evaporates, add a bit more just to keep it moist.

This is a dinner beef serving and half a dinner vegetable.

IRISH   **IRISH BRAISED CARROTS**

1 bunch tiny carrots
½ tablespoon imitation
   butter flavoring

1 chicken bouillon cube
   dissolved in 1 cup hot
   water
Dry skim milk powder

Use very young, whole carrots about 3 inches long. Coat a Teflon frypan with the butter flavoring, then add the carrots and brown them slowly, turning as needed. When brown, weigh off four-ounce portions. Roll each portion in 1/3 cup of the dry milk powder. Line a shallow baking dish with foil to make compartments separated by foil ridges. Place 4 ounce of carrots in each compartment. Pour the chicken bouillon over all. Preheat oven to 350°, then lower heat to 325° and bake 1 hour.

Each compartment holds a dinner vegetable and a glass of milk.

IRISH   **IRISH STYLE MUSHROOMS**
                    (Unlimited)

1 pound fresh mushrooms
1 chicken bouillon cube
   dissolved in 1 cup hot
   water

¼ teaspoon lemon juice
Dash pepper

Separate the mushroom caps from the stems and place them in a saucepan with the other ingrdients. Cook, covered tightly, 5 minutes, then remove cover and cook until the broth evaporates.

66

4 ounces onions, sliced thin	1 sweet red pepper, in strips
2 cloves garlic, minced	1 sweet Italian frying pepper, in strips
3 ounces raw cubed chicken	3 ounces cooked shrimp, quartered
¼ cup hot water	1 serving DW rice
¼ cup whole mixed spices Salt and pepper to taste	

In a covered Teflon pan, sauté the onion and garlic without water until tender. Add the chicken (remove any skin), raise flame and brown the cubes 5 minutes while stirring. Add the water and mixed spices. Cover and simmer, covered, 15 minutes. Add salt and pepper to taste, then the pepper strips. Simmer 10 minutes more, until chicken is tender. Now add the shrimp and DW rice, just to heat. Mix everything thoroughly and serve hot in deep dish. Use the shrimp bits on top as a garnish.

This is a dinner serving and a dinner vegetable.

DUTCH BEETS WITH APPLES DUTCH STYLE

3 ounces beets, sliced	½ teaspoon nutmeg
1 ounce onion, chopped	Salt and pepper to taste
1 tart apple, peeled and chopped	3 tablespoons vinegar
¼ teaspoon liquid non-sugar sweetener	

Combine everything but the vinegar in a saucepan and simmer, covered, 1 hour or until the mixture is a pulp. Add the vinegar and stir. Remove from heat, mash fine and serve. Marvelous with roast meats and fowl!

This is a dinner vegetable and one fruit for the day.

BELGIAN   BRAISED ENDIVE
(An unlimited, anytime food)

4 large endives	1 chicken bouillon cube dissolved in
⅛ teaspoon imitation butter flavoring	1 cup hot water

Wash the endive and dry with paper towel. Preheat a Teflon pan, add the butter flavoring and then the endive and brown on a high flame, turning endive on all sides. When brown, add the chicken bouillon. Reduce flame, cover and cook about 20 minutes, until endive is tender. Drain and serve immediately.

BELGIAN   LEMON-BRUSSELS SPROUTS

1 chicken bouillon cube
    dissolved in 1 cup
    boiling water
	⅛ teaspoon pepper
	1 tablespoon lemon juice
	½ lemon, fluted and sliced
	    lengthwise into ovals

10 ounces Brussels sprouts, frozen or fresh	
3 tablespoons parsley flakes	

Cook sprouts in the boiling chicken broth until tender. Drain. Add the parsley, pepper and lemon juice. Toss lightly, then simmer covered (about 5 minutes) until dry. Serve with fluted lemon slices for added flavor and color. Use a French-fry potato slicer to flute the lemon edge. Looks beautiful!

This recipe equals a dinner vegetable.

GERMAN   BAVARIAN EGG IN A FRAME
(Breakfast only)

1 slice white bread, enriched	Few drops imitation butter flavoring
1 egg	

Cut a circle from the center of the slice of bread, using a small glass as your guide. (Reserve the round). Preheat a Teflon pan and brown one side of the bread. Turn, crack the egg into the center and cook until egg is done. Rub a few drops of butter flavoring on the round of bread and serve on the side of your egg in a frame!

GERMAN   SWEET-AND-SOUR FISH
(Lunch or Dinner)

3 pounds fish (whitefish,
    haddock or pike)
	½ cup cold water
	½ teaspoon liquid
	    non-sugar sweetener

1 large onion, sliced	
1 large carrot, sliced	1 bay leaf

2 stalks celery, diced
    (optional)
	1 or 2 small whole
	    peppercorns

1 cup white vinegar	2 lemon slices, halved

Clean the fish, salt lightly and refrigerate overnight. Next day, simmer the onion, carrot and celery in a large saucepan, with water barely to cover, until soft (15 to 20 minutes). Set aside. Combine the vinegar, water and sweetener, adjusting the ingredients to your taste, and add this to the vegetables. Add the bay leaf and peppercorns. Now take the fish from the refrigerator, wash well to remove salt and add to the saucepan. Cook gently (avoid a rolling boil) 30 minutes, then carefully remove the fish to a platter and let cool. Strain the broth, cool, and pour it over the fish. Arrange the vegetables around the fish. Refrigerate platter uncovered until the winey broth jells. (Make this two days ahead for thorough jelling—it will keep fresh in the refrigerator an entire week and is wonderful for company dinner!) Serve over crisp lettuce, garnished with lemon slices.

Eight ounces of cooked fish with skin and bones is a dinner fish serving. For a lunch serving take four ounces of fish with skin and bone.

GERMAN   SAUERBRATEN

1 cup vinegar	1 teaspoon allspice
3 small onions, quartered	1 teaspoon rosemary
2 stalks celery (with leaves), cut up	1 teaspoon thyme
2 sprigs parsley	1 teaspoon basil
1 carrot, sliced	½ teaspoon liquid non-sugar sweetener
4 whole cloves	4 pounds round or rump roast beef
2 teaspoons peppercorns	

To make sauce: Put all the ingredients but the meat through the blender until pureéd to a marinade consistency. Place the meat in a baking dish, pour the marinade over it, cover and refrigerate 36 hours, turning meat once. To cook: Transfer the meat to a large Teflon pan and sear all sides on high flame. Return meat to the baking dish with the marinade, and in a 350° oven, roast 1 ½ hours for medium rare. Baste occasionally. For more doneness, reduce flame to 325° and bake another ½ hour. To serve, slice as a roast beef, and offer the sauce as a side dish.

Six ounces of meat, sliced, is a beef dinner serving and half a cup of sauce is a dinner vegetable.

GERMAN   SWEET AND SOUR MACKEREL

1 tablespoon liquid non-sugar sweetener	Parsley flakes
2 capfuls vinegar	Lettuce
Juice of ½ lemon	Cucumber
¼ cup water	Radishes
4 ounces onion, sliced thin	2 ounces tomato, sliced
3 large mackerel, cleaned, scaled, with head, tail and fins removed and cut in 10-ounce portions	

Make the sauce by combining the sweetener, vinegar, lemon juice and water. Stir, taste and adjust for the winey sweet-and-sour flavor you like. Set aside. In a Teflon pan, cover and cook the onions 10 minutes, until tender. Add the mackerel, lower flame, cover and simmer 20 minutes, turning the fish once. Pour sauce over the fish, then transfer both fish and sauce to a deep dish. Refrigerate until sauce jells. Serve each portion with the jellied sauce that clings to it, sprinkled with chopped parsley and on a bed of lettuce. Serve cucumber, radishes and 2 ounces of tomato slices.

Each portion is a dinner fish serving. The tomato slices and half the onion equal a dinner vegetable.

GERMAN   APPLES AND SAUERKRAUT

1 large can sauerkraut   5 or 6 eating apples

Place half of the sauerkraut from the can in a 2-quart jar. Wash the apples and add them. Fill jar with sauerkraut juice and let marinate in your refrigerator 3 or 4 days. Serve as a side dish with meat, adding sauerkraut if you like.

One apple equals a fruit for the day. The sauerkraut is unlimited—and a great TV snack.

GERMAN RED CABBAGE AND CUCUMBER SALAD
(Unlimited)

1 head red cabbage   Salt
1 cucumber,   Pepper
** sliced thin   Lemon juice**

Cut the cabbage in quarters and shred each quarter separately. Place in serving bowl. Add salt, pepper and the lemon juice to taste. Toss and serve!

GERMAN   SWEET AND SOUR GERMAN
CABBAGE CAKE

1 medium green cabbage,   ½ ounce liquid non-sugar
** shredded fine   sweetener**
1 medium apple, peeled   3 ounces water
** and sliced   Dash cinnamon**
1 ounce white vinegar

Combine the water, vinegar, sweetener, cabbage and apple in a saucepan. Cover and cook over a low flame until tender (20 to 30 minutes). Add water if liquid cooks out. To serve, top with a dash of cinnamon. A delicious side dish with chicken or turkey.

This is a fruit for the day.

SPANISH   **SPANISH GAZPACHO**
                   (Dinner only)

½ clove garlic   ½ teaspoon salt
 3 ounces tomato, peeled   ⅛ teaspoon pepper
    and chunked   1 tablespoon vinegar
¼ green pepper, diced   1 ounce onion, sliced
½ cucumber, peeled and   ½ cup cold water
    chunked

Put everything through blender. Refrigerate and serve
cold in chilled glass. A refreshing, nutritious soup. Good
all year, great for summer buffet parties.

This recipe equals a dinner vegetable.

FOR JELLIED GAZPACHO: Bring the ½ cup water to
a boil, remove from heat and soften 1 package of unflavored
gelatine in it. Stir to dissolve completely. Let cool, then put
through blender with all other ingredients and refrigerate in
a mold until jelled.

POLISH   **POLISH SOUR TOMATOES**

   Plum tomatoes, or   4 stalks celery (with
   green ones   leaves), in chunks
 2 tablespoons coarse salt
 1 tablespoon pickling
    spices

Wash the tomatoes well and place in a one-quart jar
filled ¾ with cold water. Add the salt, pickling spices and
celery. Seal the jar tight. Shake well and let stand at room
temperature 2 days, or until it begins to ferment. Loosen
cap to let air escape and then refrigerate. Serve with any
meat or fowl. This keeps indefinitely in your refrigerator.

Four ounces is a dinner vegetable.

HUNGARIAN   **CHICKEN PAPRIKASH**

2 ½ pound fryer   Pepper
  4 ounces onion, sliced   1 glass buttermilk
  1 teaspoon paprika   DW Peppered noodles
     Salt

Cut the fryer as for Southern fry. In a Teflon pan, on a
high flame, brown the onions and the chicken on both sides.
Sprinkle with paprika and salt and pepper to taste, while
browning. Add the buttermilk. Cover, reduce flame and
simmer 20 minutes, or until tender. Serve on a bed of peppered noodles.

71

One-half the chicken is a dinner serving and the vegetables and sauce equal a dinner vegetable and one glass of milk.

HUNGARIAN   GOULASH SUPREME

½ pound beef, cubed
   (trim off all fat)
½ cup tomato juice
½ teaspoon garlic powder
¼ teaspoon salt (optional)
4 ounces carrots
1 chicken bouillon cube,
   dissolved in ½ cup
   water

1 green pepper, diced
½ teaspoon paprika
   Dash black pepper
½ can mushrooms
½ can La Choy bean
   sprouts
½ can French-style string
   beans
½ box frozen cauliflower
   (let thaw)

Place all ingredients except the canned vegetables and the cauliflower in a stewing pot. Cover and simmer one hour. Drain all vegetables and add them, stirring well. Cover and simmer 30 minutes, or until meat is tender to a fork test. Cool, then refrigerate. Skim off all congealed fat. Reheat to serve.

The entire dish is one dinner beef serving and a dinner vegetable.

HUNGARIAN   SAUSAGE GOULASH

2 ounces onion, diced
1 can bean sprouts,
   drained well
¼ teaspoon caraway seeds
2 ounces tomato, peeled
   and mashed

½ teaspoon paprika
   Pinch salt
8 ounces frankfurters,
   sliced crosswise
   into quarters

In a covered Teflon frypan, sauté the onion over a small flame until tender (about 5 minutes). Remove cover, raise flame, add bean sprouts and continue cooking until onion is golden brown. Add caraway seeds, tomato, paprika, salt and franks. Cover and simmer until franks are tender. Stir occasionally and add ¼ cup water if necessary.

This equals a dinner beef serving and a dinner vegetable.

HUNGARIAN DW PEPPERED NOODLES
(Unlimited)

2 cans bean sprouts
1 green pepper, diced fine
1 red pepper, diced fine

¼ cup tomato juice
   Parsley
   Garlic powder

In a Teflon pan, combine the bean sprouts, peppers and tomato juice. Cover and cook 10 minutes on a medium flame. Remove cover and raise the flame to cook out the rest of the tomato juice. Sprinkle with parsley. When ready to serve, add a dash of garlic powder.

HUNGARIAN SWEET AND SOUR CABBAGE

4 ounces onion, diced
1 medium cabbage, shredded (red or green)
1 medium apple, peeled and sliced

1 ounce white vinegar
½ ounce liquid non-sugar sweetener
3 ounces water

Saute' onion in covered Teflon pan until soft and translucent (the onion will release its own liquid). Remove cover and raise flame to brown the onion just slightly. Add a layer of shredded cabbage and the apples. Pour the other ingredients over all. Cover and cook over small flame until cabbage is tender (20 to 30 minutes). Check occasionally for sauce. If it cooks out, add water.

EASY WAY TO SHRED CABBAGE FINE: Wash cabbage and cut in quarters. With sharp knife shred each quarter separately.

This recipe equals one fruit for the day and one serving of a dinner vegetable.

RUMANIAN   RUMANIAN LATKIS
(Breakfast only)

1 slice white bread
1 egg
2 ounces skim milk
Salt

Pepper
4 ounces canned mushrooms, sliced

Toast the bread well and put it through the blender together with the raw egg, milk, and salt and pepper to taste. Pour this batter into a preheated Teflon frypan. Drain the sliced mushrooms and place them on the batter. Fry on one side, turn carefully and fry the second side.

RUMANIAN   RUMANIAN BROILED
TENDERLOIN

1 tenderloin steak
3 or 4 cloves garlic, mashed fine with mallet or garlic press

Score the steak in a criss-cross pattern on both sides and place the crushed garlic cloves in the ridges. Broil about 5 minutes on each side for medium rare. Slice at an angle.

Six ounces is a dinner beef serving.

RUMANIAN RUMANIAN MUSCHI STEAK

Two-inch thick fillet of steak
3 or 4 cloves garlic, crushed well
Cooked cauliflower, mashed fine

1 ounce onion, sliced
½ pound fresh mushrooms
Lettuce
3 ounces tomato, sliced

In a covered Teflon pan sauté the onion, then remove cover and raise flame to brown. Set aside. Score the steak and place the crushed garlic in the ridges. Broil 2 inches from flame, 7 to 8 minutes on each side for medium rare. Separate the mushroom caps and broil them with the steak. Serve the steak topped with the French fried onion, and with the mashed cauliflower and mushrooms on the side. Add a salad of lettuce and tomato slices.

Six ounces of steak is a dinner beef serving and the onion and tomato slices equal one dinner vegetable.

RUMANIAN EGGPLANT VINETE

1 eggplant
1 onion, chopped fine
2 or 3 peppers, chopped fine
White or black pepper
Garlic powder

1 capful of vinegar
Salt and pepper, to taste
Lettuce leaves
Radishes
Cucumber, sliced thin

Wrap the eggplant in foil and roast in a 350° oven, or on top of the stove in a potato baker until soft. Turn once to allow about 15 minutes on each side. When tender, remove foil and let heat escape. When cool, peel it with your fingers. Chop entire eggplant in a chopping bowl, then add the onion and mix. Combine the green and red peppers in a separate dish. Weigh off 4 ounces of eggplant-onion mixture and combine this with 1 or 2 tablespoons of the chopped peppers, a dash of garlic and a capful of vinegar. Add salt and pepper. Mix well. Serve on a flat dish on crisp lettuce, with sliced red radishes (or, as the Rumanians do, use white radish) and thin cucumber slices.

Four ounces are a dinner vegetable.

SICILIAN   VEAL AND ZUCCHINI

8 ounces veal scallopini or stewing veal	⅛ teaspoon basil leaves
2 green or red peppers, in strips	⅛ teaspoon garlic powder
¼ cup tomato juice	½ teaspoon parsley
4 ounces zucchini, sliced	¼ teaspoon white or black pepper
⅛ teaspoon oregano	½ pound cooked fresh mushrooms or 1 large can

Sear the veal in a Teflon pan, with the peppers. Add the tomato juice, zucchini, oregano, basil, garlic powder, parsley and pepper. Cover and cook on medium flame until meat is tender. Five minutes before it's done, add the drained mushrooms, just to heat them.

This recipe is a dinner meat serving, a dinner vegetable and ¼ cup of tomato juice.

GREEK   GRILLED LEMON COD
(Lunch Psari—Greek for fish)

4 ounces cod	Dill
Paprika	½ lemon
Parsley	

Sprinkle the cod with the paprika, parsley and dill. Squeeze juice of ½ lemon over it. Preheat broiler and broil 2 or 3 minutes on each side. Serve!

This is a lunch fish serving.

GREEK   AEGEAN CASSEROLE
(Dinner)

8 ounce can sliced mushrooms	6 ounces cooked lamb
¾ cup tomato juice	½ teaspoon parsley
½ ounce onion, diced	Dash salt
3 ½ ounces carrots, sliced diagonally	

Drain mushrooms and put half through blender with the tomato juice and onion to make a sauce. Add sliced mushrooms. Combine this with all the rest of the ingredients in a casserole. Bake in 325° oven until carrots are tender.

This is a dinner meat serving, a dinner vegetable and 6 ounces of tomato juice for the day.

GREEK   **BEEFSTEAKS**
(Dinner)

1 pound beef, ground
4 ounces onion, chopped
½ teaspoon salt
¼ teaspoon lemon peel, grated

½ tablespoon lemon juice
½ teaspoon dried mint flakes

Place all ingredients in a mixing bowl and mix. Wetting your hands with cold water, shape mixture into thick flat patties. Preheat broiler and broil 7 minutes on one side, turn and broil 5 minutes on other side for medium rare. Increase or decrease the broiling time according to your preference for "doneness".

Six ounces cooked equals one dinner beef serving and two ounces of a dinner vegetable.

GREEK   **MUSHROOMS**
(Unlimited)

½ teaspoon imitation butter flavoring
1 ½ tablespoons wine vinegar
Dash parsley
Marjoram
Dash salt

1 bay leaf
1 clove garlic, diced
½ cup water
1 pound small fresh mushroom caps

Combine the butter flavoring, vinegar, herbs and water in a saucepan. Simmer gently. When herbs are tender, remove them and continue to cook the sauce slowly until it is reduced to half. Add the mushrooms and cook 5 minutes more. Chill and serve cold.

GREEK   **GREEK SALAD**
(Unlimited)

¼ cup vinegar
¼ cup lemon juice
Liquid non-sugar sweetener to taste
½ cup water
¼ head lettuce, cut up

¼ head cabbage, shredded
1 green pepper, diced fine
1 red pepper, diced fine
Salt
Pepper
½ teaspoon parsley flakes

Combine the vinegar, lemon juice, sweetener and water for dressing. Mix together the lettuce, cabbage and peppers. Pour dressing over the vegetables and marinate 3 hours. Add a dash salt and pepper, and the parsley, then chill. Drain and serve.

76

SKOL IN SCANDINAVIA

BREAKFAST

SWEDISH STEAMED EGGS
(Breakfast only)

1 egg
½ cup skim milk

Pinch salt
1 slice white bread

Break egg into mixing bowl and add the milk and salt. Beat until light and fluffy. Cook in double boiler 10 minutes or until like a custard. *Do not stir*. Serve at once over a slice of warm toast.

This recipe equals one half cup of milk for the day.

LUNCH OR DINNER

SWEDISH SWEET AND SOUR SALMON
(A quickie)

1 can salmon
  (7-ounce), drained
1 tablespoon white
  vinegar
1 teaspoon liquid
  non-sugar sweetener

2 ounces onion,
  diced fine
2 ounces tomato

Combine the salmon, vinegar, sweetener and onion, mixing well. Serve on a large bed of crisp lettuce with the sliced tomato and all the unlimited vegetables you like.

This recipe equals one dinner fish serving plus one dinner vegetable.

FOR LUNCH: Use 3 ¾ ounces of salmon and just half of all other ingredients. *Substitute* 2 ounces of celery (diced fine) for the onion, and thin cucumber slices for the tomato. Add two or three strips of pimiento.

DINNERS

SPICY SMORGASBORD SHRIMP

½ pound shrimp
⅓ cup white vinegar
½ teaspoon garlic powder
½ teaspoon dehydrated
   dill, or 3 or 4 fresh
   sprigs

1 bay leaf
Dash pepper

Shell, devein and wash shrimp well. Place in saucepan with vinegar, garlic, seasonings. Cook 15 to 20 minutes, just until shrimp is tender (do not overcook). Chill, strain and serve with picks, garnishing with parsley.

Six ounces of shrimp is a dinner serving and four ounces is a lunch serving.

SMORGASBORD FISH BALLS

3 ½ pounds pike and
   whitefish, ground
   together
2 eggs
1 small onion, diced fine
2 drops liquid non-sugar
   sweetener

Salt and pepper to taste
2 ½ cups water
2 carrots, sliced
   diagonally
2 or 3 celery stalks, diced

Have your fish dealer grind the fish and pack head, bones and other scraps separately to take with you. Place the ground fish, eggs, onion, sweetener, salt and pepper in a large chopping bowl and chop very fine, gradually adding ½ cup of water. When mixture is light and fluffy, moisten both hands with cold water and shape into tiny (1 inch) balls. Set aside. Place fish scraps on bottom of a saucepan and cover them with the carrot and celery. Add two cups of water and bring rapidly to a boil. Lower flame, cover pot and cook ¾ hour, until carrots and celery are tender. Then remove cover, raise flame. As the water boils up, gently lower the fish balls over the bed of vegetables. Re-cover and simmer 2 hours. If water boils out, add more so you have a gravy at the end. Serve with a side dish of horseradish. Delicious hot (over a candle warmer) or cold, in a deep bowl with tiny skewers.

Serve carrots and celery cold as a separate dish.

Six ounces of fish equal a dinner portion and 3 ounces are a lunch portion. Four ounces of carrots equal a dinner vegetable.

SMORGASBORD SWORDFISH

3 pounds swordfish
1 large onion, sliced
1 large carrot, sliced
2 stalks celery, diced
1 cup white vinegar

½ cup cold water
½ teaspoon liquid
  non-sugar sweetener
1 bay leaf
1 or 2 whole peppercorns

Simmer the onion, carrot and celery in a large saucepan, with water barely to cover, until soft (15 to 20 minutes), and set aside. Combine the vinegar, water and sweetener, adjusting this to your taste, and add it to the vegetables. Add the bay leaf, peppercorns, and swordfish (carefully) and cook *gently* 30 minutes. Then carefully remove the fish to a platter and let it cool. Strain the broth, cool, and pour it over the fish. Refrigerate the platter uncovered until the broth jells well. To serve, cut into 1 ½-inch cubes leaving some jelly around each cube. Skewer with small picks and serve in a deep bowl.

Arrange vegetables in a separate bowl and chill them also with some broth. Serve jelled.

Six ounces of cubed fish equals one dinner fish serving. Use small amount of jellied vegetable just as a garnish.

SIDE DISHES

CUCUMBER-ONION SALAD

¼ cup vinegar
2 tablespoons water
¼ teaspoon salt
½ teaspoon liquid
  non-sugar sweetener
Dash paprika

Dash black pepper
1 cucumber
4 ounces onion, sliced
  into rings
1 teaspoon parsley

Combine first six ingredients for marinade. Slice the cucumber thin (do not peel), mix with onion rings and marinate 4 hours. Serve chilled on Smorgasbord table or as salad for any main dish. Top with parsley.

This is a luscious dinner vegetable.

MARINATED CELERY CHUNKS
(Unlimited)

Celery stalks cut into
  chunks
4 tablespoons vinegar
2 tablespoons water
1 clove garlic, diced

½ teaspoon salt
⅛ teaspoon paprika
½ teaspoon non-sugar
  liquid sweetener

Combine all ingredients and let the celery marinate 3 hours. Drain and serve on Smorgasbord table or as a side dish.

SMORGASBORD BEET AND ONION SALAD

2 ounces canned beets, diced fine
2 ounces onion, sliced thin
1 teaspoon tarragon
Dash salt
Dash pepper

½ teaspoon liquid non-sugar sweetener
1 teaspoon parsley
1 teaspoon thyme
1 teaspoon water

Combine all ingredients, chill and serve on Smorgasbord table or as a side dish.

This recipe is a dinner vegetable.

SMORGASBORD MUSHROOM BOWL
(Unlimited)

1 pound fresh mushrooms
Dash soy sauce
2 chicken bouillon cubes dissolved in 2 cups water

Wash mushrooms but do not separate stems. Cook in soy sauce and chicken bouillon just until softened. Drain and chill. Serve in a pretty bowl.

RUSSIAN HOLIDAY

LUNCH

POACHED PIKE WITH MUSHROOM STUFFING
(A quickie lunch or dinner)

1 pike
Paprika
Garlic powder
Parsley

½ pound fresh mushrooms
1 bouillon cube dissolved
   in 1 cup hot water
1 slice white toast

Have your fish dealer clean and scale the pike, trim head, tail, fins, slit the belly and cut the fish into 5-ounce portions. At home, rub the outside with paprika, garlic and parsley. Slice the mushrooms and stuff them into the belly, closing with skewers. Bring the bouillon to a boil in a saucepan, reduce flame and add the fish. Cover and simmer 10 minutes. Serve in a soup bowl over a slice of toast.

A five-ounce portion is a lunch serving. Two 5-ounce portions (omit toast) are a dinner serving.

DINNERS

BAKED STUFFED FISH

1 cup tomato juice
1 clove garlic, minced
  (or ½ teaspoon garlic
  powder)

4 fish fillets to equal
  ½ pound (any fish you
  like)
Salt and pepper, to taste

Pour tomato juice into baking pan. Pat fish dry and sprinkle with garlic, salt, pepper. Top each fillet with one tablespoon of mushroom-pepper stuffing and roll up carefully, fastening with small picks. Place stuffed fillets 1 inch apart in baking pan. In 350° oven bake 30 minutes. Serve garnished with lemon wedges.

This equals one dinner fish serving and one cup of tomato juice.

MUSHROOM-PEPPER STUFFING

¾ pound fresh mush-
  rooms, or ¾ can,
  drained
1 ounce onion, diced
½ teaspoon salt (optional)

1 green pepper, diced
Dash cayenne pepper
A few drops tomato
juice

Chop the canned mushrooms, or boil fresh ones in a covered Teflon pan without water until tender, and then drain and chop. Add onion, salt, the diced green pepper and cayenne powder. Sauté this mixture in a few drops of tomato juice just to soften the pepper. Let cool and chop fine. Delicious for stuffing fish or veal.

This equals one ounce of a dinner vegetable.

BEEF STROGANOFF

8 ounces filet of beef
(any kind)
Salt
⅛ teaspoon pepper
2 ounces small sweet
onion, diced fine
½ pound fresh mushrooms,
washed and sliced

Pinch dry or prepared
mustard (hot or sweet)
4 ounces buttermilk
blended with 2 ounces
fresh tomato

Trim all fat from beef and cut into thin strips 2 inches long. Sprinkle lightly with salt and pepper and set aside. Put onion in Teflon pan and sauté until golden brown, then add the mushrooms and beef slices and sauté five minutes more. Mix mustard well with the creamed tomato purée and pour over meat. Simmer, covered, ten minutes or until meat is tender. Refrigerate. Skim off fat and reheat. Serve in a deep dish.

This recipe equals a dinner beef serving, one dinner vegetable and half a glass of milk.

SOUPS, SIDE DISHES, SNACKS AND SAUCES

CREAMED BORSCHT

1 large can sliced beets,
or 1 bunch fresh
1 ½ cups water
2 to 3 teaspoons lemon
juice
Dash salt
Dash pepper

Giblets of 1 chicken
2 teaspoons liquid
non-sugar sweetener
1 clove garlic, or ½
teaspoon garlic powder
1 small onion, sliced
Buttermilk

Cook all the ingredients together (except the buttermilk) until giblets are tender (about 30 minutes). The mixture should taste winey. Allow to cool, then refrigerate. To make it a creamed borscht, combine ½ glass of borscht with ½ glass of buttermilk. Shake well and serve in a bowl.

One glass equals one dinner vegetable plus half a glass of milk.

MOCK BORSCHT

4 ounces buttermilk　　　　**4 ounces tomato juice**

Combine in a jar or cocktail shaker, shake up and drink up!

This recipe equals half a glass of milk and four ounces of tomato juice.

OLD-RUSSIAN BORSCHT

2 bouillon cubes　　　　　　**Dash salt**
4 cups boiling water　　　　**Dash pepper**
½ cup grated raw beets　　　**Cucumber slices**
2 tablespoons lemon juice

Dissolve bouillon cubes in boiling water. Add the grated beets and cook in a covered saucepan 15 minutes. Let cool, then refrigerate. Add lemon juice just before serving. Add salt and pepper to taste. Garnish with cucumber slices.

Each serving equals one dinner vegetable.

MUSHROOM SOUP

2 ounces onion, diced　　　　**½ pound fresh mushrooms,**
2 ounces carrots, diced　　　　**washed and sliced**
1 cup celery, diced　　　　　**1 chicken bouillon cube**
1 cup cauliflowerettes　　　**1 ½ cups water**
1 teaspoon parsley　　　　　**Salt and pepper, to taste**

In a large covered Teflon pan, sauté the onions, then lift cover and raise flame to brown. Add the rest of the ingredients. Cover and let cook 45 minutes on small flame until all vegetables are tender. Serve hot on a cold winter night.

This recipe equals one dinner vegetable.

SCHAV OR SOUR GRASS
(A drink—unlimited)

1 pound sorrel leaves　　　　**8 glasses cold water**
(also called sour grass,　　　**Salt to taste (about**
or schav)　　　　　　　　　**1 tablespoon)**

Remove leaves from stems and wash well under cold running water to remove all sand. Drain. Taking a handful at a time, shred leaves with a very sharp knife, then place in large pot. Wash stems thoroughly and select only the thick ones, which have the flavor (discard the scrawny ones). Tie stems into a bunch, winding white sewing thread around them lightly several times. Place stems on top of leaves in pot. Add cold water and salt, bring to a boil, then reduce heat and simmer, covered, 5 minutes. Discard tied stems. Let schav cool. Pour into jars and refrigerate. A truly refreshing cold drink.

MUSHROOMS AFTER CHEKHOV
(Unlimited)

½ **pound fresh mushrooms**   **Salt**

Choose large mushrooms in peak condition. Refrigerate to chill. Wash well and cut off dried end of stem. Slice lengthwise in ¼ inch wide strips that include cap and stem. Place in serving bowl and salt generously. Serve.

Unlimited and delicious as an hors d'oeuvre. Try it with unlimited DW drinks while others in the party are eating the fattening things.

SWEET AND SOUR SALAD DRESSING
(Unlimited)

4 **tablespoons vinegar**   ⅛ **teaspoon paprika**
2 **tablespoons water**   ½ **teaspoon liquid**
1 **clove garlic, diced**   **non-sugar sweetener**
½ **teaspoon salt**

Combine all ingredients and chill in refrigerator. This makes a delicious marinade or dressing for vegetables such as cucumber slices, cauliflowerettes or celery sticks—or for any tossed salad.

MIDDLE EASTERN INTRIGUE

LUNCH

TUNA CURRY
(Lunch only)

1 can (3 ¾ ounce) tuna, drained
½ teaspoon curry powder
½ cup skim milk
½ teaspoon ground ginger
1 tablespoon lemon juice
¼ teaspoon salt
1 slice bread, toasted

Flake the tuna. Combine with all other ingredients (except bread) and heat. Serve over the slice of bread, toasted.

This recipe equals one lunch fish serving and ½ cup of milk for the day.

DINNERS

ARMENIAN LAMB

1 pound breast of lamb
Paprika
Garlic powder
Prepared mustard

Trim all fat from lamb carefully and cut into strips like spare ribs. Coat with paprika and garlic powder, then rub with prepared mustard. Broil far from flame on both sides until meat is well done (about 10 minutes on each side). Serve with Eggplant-Zucchini surprise as a side dish (see index).

Ten ounces of lamb equal one dinner beef serving.

ORIENTAL CHICKEN

½ cup Dole's chunked pineapple (packed without sugar)
2 chicken bouillon cubes dissolved in 2 cups hot water
½ cup pineapple juice
½ cup dry powered skim milk
¼ teaspoon salt
¼ teaspoon Tabasco sauce
6 ounces cubed chicken, cooked
½ cup diced celery
2 tablespoons green pepper, chopped
1 pimiento, chopped
¼ teaspoon sesame seeds

In a covered Teflon pan, sauté pineapple 5 minutes. Add the chicken broth and bring to a boil. Add the pineapple juice and dry milk, stirring to dissolve the powder as it cooks (about 1 minute). Now add the salt, Tabasco sauce, green pepper and pimiento, cover and cook 5 minutes more. Serve over DW sautéed noodles and top with sesame seeds.

This recipe equals a dinner chicken serving, two fruits and a glass of milk.

CURRIED CHICKEN

3 **pound chicken, quartered (fryer or broiler)**	⅛ **teaspoon cayenne pepper**
1 **cup celery, chopped fine**	¼ **teaspoon salt**
4 **ounces onion, diced fine**	**Dash black pepper**
1 **tablespoon curry powder**	1 **cup boiling water DW rice**
2 **apples, pared, cored, quartered**	

In covered Teflon pan, cook chicken 10 minutes with skin side down, then remove cover and raise flame to brown the chicken. Remove chicken and drain all liquid, wiping pan with paper towel. Place celery and onion in Teflon pan, cover and sauté 5 minutes. Add the curry, apples, cayenne, salt and pepper, and finally the chicken. Cover and simmer 30 minutes. Add the boiling water and simmer 30 minutes more. To serve: Make DW rice, pouring the sauce over it and top each rice serving with ½ chicken.

This recipe equals two dinner servings and a dinner vegetable. Four quarters of cooked apple equal a fruit for the day.

CURRIED SHRIMP BAKE

1 **small can mushrooms**	1 **red pepper, diced**
⅓ **cup dry skim milk**	1 **large head cauliflower**
¼ **teaspoon curry powder**	
6 **ounces shrimp, cooked and diced**	

In a bowl, mix the mushrooms and their liquid with the powdered milk. Add the curry powder and taste. When it is piquant enough, add shrimp and the diced pepper, and set aside. Overcook the cauliflower, drain well and mash it fine. In a casserole place the cauliflower on the bottom.

Pour the shrimp and curry sauce mixture over the cauliflower and bake in 350° oven for ½ hour.

This dish equals one dinner seafood serving and one glass of milk for the day.

EASTERN STUFFED EGGPLANT

A medium eggplant
(about 1 pound)
1 ounce onion, diced
2 cloves garlic, minced
¼ pound ground beef
¼ pound ground lamb
DW rice

1 tablespoon parsley
2 tablespoons tomato
juice
3 drops vinegar
Pinch cinnamon
Pinch curry powder

Halve the eggplant and scrape pulp out (do not break the skin). Set shells aside. Weigh off 3 ounces of pulp and seeds and sauté this amount with the onion 5 minutes in a covered Teflon pan. Remove cover and raise flame to brown the mixture. Combine with all the rest of the ingredients and chop thoroughly to aerate. Stuff this mixture into eggplant shells, mounding the top neatly. Place stuffed shells in small pan with ¼ cup water. Cover pan tightly with aluminum foil and bake 40 minutes in 350° oven. Remove foil and cook uncovered 5 minutes more.

Both shells equal one dinner beef serving plus a dinner vegetable and 2 ounces of tomato juice.

Save uncooked eggplant pulp for DW Mideastern Leftover Surprise.

LAMB CURRY

3 pounds stewing lamb
⅓ cup dry powdered skim
milk
2 cloves garlic, diced
4 ounces onion, sliced
2 apples, pared and
quartered
4 tablespoons curry
2 tablespoons liquid
non-sugar sweetener

2 tablespoons Worcester-
shire sauce
2 lemons, sliced
½ teaspoon grated lime
peel
1 pound whole mushrooms
½ teaspoon salt
1 cup boiling water
1 summer squash

Cut the lamb into 2-inch cubes and roll in the dry powdered milk. Sauté the garlic and onion in a covered Teflon pan 5 minutes. Remove cover and raise flame to brown onion lightly. Add meat and cook 10 minutes, stirring well. Brown meat only lightly. Now add the apples and curry and simmer 5 minutes, stirring occasionally. Finally, add everything else but the squash (raise flame so water continues to boil, then reduce flame). Cover and simmer 1 hour. About 5 minutes before serving, wash summer squash well, slice very thin and add to the sauce to heat.

Six ounces of lamb equal dinner beef serving. The sauce has a glass of milk and a dinner vegetable. Four apple quarters are a fruit.

SCALLOP AND SHRIMP CURRY

1 pound scallops, washed and halved

1 pound shrimp, shelled, washed, deveined

4 ounces onion, chopped

1 tablespoon curry powder, or to taste

½ cup skim milk

⅓ cup dry skim milk powder

1 teaspoon ground ginger

3 tablespoons lemon juice

1 teaspoon salt

Summer squash

Parsley flakes

Sauté onion in Teflon saucepan 5 minutes. Add the curry powder, skim milk and dry milk powder. Cook over very low flame, stirring to dissolve the milk powder. Add the scallops and shrimp, ginger, lemon juice and salt. Simmer uncovered for 30 minutes, stirring frequently. Make DW Rice and heat in ½ cup of the pan sauce. Transfer rice to platter and top with the shrimp and scallops. Wash a summer squash, dice it fine or grate, and sprinkle each serving with it (tastes like "coconut!"). Add a dash of parsley flakes.

Six ounces of shrimp and scallops combined are a dinner seafood serving. One half cup of the sauce is one half glass of milk and two ounces of a dinner vegetable.

SHISH KABOB

8 ounces boned shoulder of lamb

1 cup vinegar

½ teaspoon cinnamon

1 ½ teaspoons cloves

1 ounce onion, diced

1 clove garlic, diced fine

½ teaspoon parsley

Dash paprika

½ pound fresh mushrooms

1 green pepper, cubed

3 ounces tomato, sliced

Make a marinade by heating the vinegar, cinnamon and cloves. Let this cool and add the onion, garlic, parsley and a dash of paprika. Cube the lamb and marinate it overnight in the sauce. To cook, skewer the lamb, mushrooms, green pepper and tomato slices in that order and broil in your oven or on an outdoor grill. Turn to brown both sides until they are well done. Serve with a tossed salad and, if you like, DW Rice.

This recipe equals a dinner beef serving and a dinner vegetable.

TURKISH KABOBS

½ **pound beef tenderloin**	**DW rice**
½ **pound fresh mushrooms**	¼ **cup tomato juice**
Bay leaves	1 **tablespoon parsley**
Salt	**flakes**
Pepper	**Dash curry powder**

Cube the beef. Wash mushrooms and on skewers, alternate: A mushroom, beef cube, bay leaf, repeating until used up. Sprinkle with salt and pepper. Line broiler with foil, place skewers on it and broil 2 inches from flame for 7 minutes on each side, turning once. Make DW rice, heating it in the tomato juice seasoned with parsley and curry powder. Drain, transfer to serving platter and top with the Turkish kabobs.

This recipe equals one dinner beef serving.

SOUPS, SIDE DISHES, SNACKS AND SAUCES

ARMENIAN GREEN SOUP

2 **tablespoons diced green pepper**	4 **ounces scallion or onion**
½ **teaspoon salt**	½ **teaspoon celery seeds (optional)**
1 **large cucumber, unpeeled, diced**	¼ **teaspoon white pepper**
2 **tablespoons parsley flakes**	¼ **teaspoon dill seeds**
	1 **quart buttermilk**

In a bowl or large jar, combine all the ingredients. Chill thoroughly. Serve in bowls garnished with very thin slices of unpeeled cucumber.

An eight-ounce bowl equals one glass of milk and one ounce of a dinner vegetable. This is a great soup for a hot night. Store in a jar in your refrigerator and enjoy it as a snack too!

APPLE-CABBAGE CHUTNEY

1 **medium red cabbage, shredded fine**	2 **ounces grape flavor No-Cal syrup**
1 **medium apple, peeled and sliced**	3 **ounces water**
1 **ounce white vinegar**	**Dash nutmeg**

Mix the water, vinegar and grape syrup. Place in a saucepan with the cabbage and apple. Cover and cook over a low flame until tender (20 to 30 minutes). If liquid cooks out, add water. Just before serving, sprinkle top with nutmeg. Try this with all curry dishes!

The entire recipe equals one fruit for the day.

CURRIED CABBAGE
(Unlimited)

1 medium cabbage, coarsely shredded	½ teaspoon curry powder ½ cup water

Place the shredded cabbage in a Teflon pan. Add the curry powder and water and mix. Bring to a boil. Cover and simmer until liquid evaporates. The cabbage will be tender but crisp.

DW PEPPER CHUTNEY

2 ounces chopped onion ½ cup green pepper, chopped 2 ounces tomatoes, peeled and chopped	¼ cup sweet red pepper, chopped ¼ cup lemon juice

Combine all ingredients and let stand at room temperature 1 hour, stirring frequently. Serve.

This recipe is a dinner vegetable.

HOT LEMON CHUTNEY
(Unlimited, very hot and definitely a make-ahead chutney)

4 lemons, each cut into six wedges 3 tablespoons salt 4 tablespoons crushed dry red pepper	¼ teaspoon garlic powder 1 teaspoon paprika ⅛ teaspoon imitation butter flavoring

Roll each lemon wedge in salt. Marinate at room temperature 4 days. Heat the butter flavoring in a Teflon pan and pour over the lemons. Add the red pepper, garlic powder and paprika. Let cool, cover, and marinate at room temperature another 4 days. Serve.

MADRAS CUCUMBER CHUTNEY

6 small sweet summer cucumbers Salt 1 clove garlic, chopped fine 1 tablespoon pimiento, diced 2 stalks celery, diced	1 tablespoon parsley flakes ¼ teaspoon black pepper Pinch cayenne 2 tablespoons lemon juice Dash salt 2 tablespoons buttermilk (optional)

Pare and salt the cucumbers and let stand 1 hour. Wash off salt and then dice them. Combine with all the other ingredients. Perfect for curry dishes that already contain a dinner vegetable.

This recipe equals 2 tablespoons of milk for the day, if you use the buttermilk.

MAJOR LEE'S PINEAPPLE CHUTNEY

½ **fresh pineapple, cut
   into small chunks**
½ **cup water**
2 **drops mint extract**
2 **drops peppermint
   extract**

½ **teaspoon liquid
   non-sugar sweetener**
3 **drops yellow vegetable
   coloring**
4 **drops red vegetable
   coloring**

Combine the ingredients and chill. Serve with lamb and chicken dishes, or as a snack.

This recipe is a fruit for the day.

MID-EASTERN LEFTOVER SURPRISE

Leftover eggplant pulp
3 **ounces onion, diced**
Dash curry

1 **teaspoon parsley**
Dash paprika
1 **ounce tomato juice**

Cube eggplant and set aside. In Teflon pan sauté onion 5 minutes, then raise cover and brown. Add curry, parsley, paprika, the eggplant cubes and tomato juice. Simmer covered until tomato juice evaporates and eggplant is tender.

Four ounces is a dinner vegetable.

NEAR EASTERN ARTICHOKES
(A different first course)

1 ½ **pounds artichokes**
  1 **teaspoon cider vinegar**
  1 **tablespoon parsley
     flakes**

⅛ **teaspoon imitation
   butter flavoring**

Wash and scrape the artichokes, and cook in boiling water to cover until tender to a fork test (about 15 minutes). Drain and slice. Combine the vinegar, parsley and butter flavoring and pour this sauce over the artichoke slices.

This equals one dinner vegetable.

NEAR EASTERN MUSHROOMS WITH HERBS

4 ounces chopped chives, or onions chopped fine

¼ teaspoon (optional) imitation butter flavoring

1 pound sliced fresh mushrooms or 1 can, drained

¼ cup chicken bouillon

1 tablespoon chopped parsley

1 teaspoon marjoram

Cook the chives or onions in the butter flavoring until lightly browned. Add the mushrooms, tossing to coat them well. Add the chicken bouillon, the parsley and marjoram. Mix and transfer to a baking dish. Bake in preheated 350° oven 20 minutes.

This recipe equals one dinner vegetable. It is excellent with meat or chicken.

EXOTICS OF THE FAR EAST
(Japan, China, Hawaii)

JAPANESE   CHICKEN-CUCUMBER SOUP DINNER
(A great leftover meal)

1 chicken bouillon cube
1 cup hot water
4 ounces bamboo shoots
   Dash soy sauce
1 small can sliced mush-
   rooms, drained

6 ounces cooked shredded
   chicken, or turkey
   white meat
½ cucumber

Simmer all ingredients but cucumber 20 minutes over a low flame. Slice cucumbers (do not peel) into ½ inch rounds, add them and boil rapidly 3 or 4 minutes longer. Serve!

This recipe equals one dinner chicken serving and one dinner vegetable.

JAPANESE   RIBLET SURPRISE

3 pounds lamb riblets
4 ounces orange juice
¼ cup Kikkoman soy
   sauce

½ tablespoon white
   horseradish
1 teaspoon prepared
   mustard

Have butcher cut lamb riblets as for spare ribs and trim as much fat as possible. At home combine the orange juice, soy sauce, horseradish and mustard. Let lamb marinate in this overnight in refrigerator, in a roasting pan covered with Saran wrap. Next day remove riblets to broiler rack and brown on both sides to cook out more fat. Return riblets to roasting pan with the marinade and in 350° oven roast 45 minutes, or until tender. Baste occasionally with marinade and turn once at the half-hour mark.

Serve this with a spicy mixture of mushrooms, bean sprouts, French-style string beans and 2 stalks of Chinese cabbage—all sliced, heated, drained, seasoned with white pepper and garlic powder, and tossed lightly.

This entire recipe equals one beef dinner serving and one fruit.

LAMB RIBS TERIYAKI

3 or 4 pounds breast of
lamb
1 clove garlic, diced
very fine
1 teaspoon ginger
1 teaspoon salt

2 teaspoons liquid
non-sugar sweetener
3 tablespoons soy sauce
1 tablespoon lemon juice
½ cup vinegar

Trim all fat off lamb, then boil lamb 10 minutes in water to cover, to remove more fat. Drain water and let lamb cool. Cut into racks and marinate in all the other ingredients overnight in your refrigerator. When ready to cook, pre-heat oven 350°. Lift ribs from marinade and arrange them on a rack in a shallow roasting pan, meat side up. Roast 1 hour, then remove ribs from oven. Drain any fat from the roasting pan drippings and add the marinating sauce. Place ribs in the marinade, spooning some over them to moisten them. Roast another half hour, until ribs are tender and well browned.

Ten ounces of cooked lamb are a dinner beef serving.

JAPANESE ## LEMON FISH

¼ cup lemon juice
¾ cup water
1 ½ teaspoons pickling spices

¼ teaspoon salt
2 pieces of swordfish, 8
ounces each

In Teflon pan combine the lemon juice, water, pickling spices and salt. Heat just to simmering. Add the swordfish, cover and simmer until fish is tender to fork test (10 to 15 minutes). That's all! Can be frozen for future meals.

Each eight-ounce portion equals one dinner seafood serving. Four ounces are a lunch serving.

JAPANESE ## SCALLOPS TEMPURA

½ tablespoon soy sauce
⅓ cup dry powdered
skim milk
½ tablespoon vinegar
(optional)

⅛ teaspoon powdered
mustard
1 egg white, beaten with
beater until stiff
8 ounces scallops

Put the soy sauce, powdered milk, vinegar and powdered mustard through the blender. Pour the mixture into a bowl and fold in the beaten egg white. Add scallops, mixing them well in this batter. Cover broiler rack with aluminum foil and arrange scallops on it. Broil 2 inches from flame 10 minutes, turning when brown. If batter burns, lower the rack.

This equals one dinner seafood serving and one glass milk for the day.

JAPANESE   TERIYAKI STEAK

2 teaspoons powdered ginger	1 teaspoon liquid non-sugar sweetener
4 ounces onion, diced	¼ cup water
½ cup soy sauce	½ pound steak (London broil or tenderloin)
2 cloves garlic, diced	

Combine the first six ingredients and pour over the steak in a suitable bowl for marinating. Marinate the meat 2 to 4 hours. Broil the steak 3 to 5 minutes on each side, depending on your preference for doneness. To serve, slice thinly at an angle, perpendicular to the grain.

This equals one dinner beef serving and a dinner vegetable.

DINNERS

CHINESE   MANDARIN SPARE RIBS

1 clove garlic, mashed	½ cup hot water
½ cup soy sauce	1 cup vinegar
¼ cup No-Cal orange syrup	1 chicken bouillon cube
¼ teaspoon white pepper	¼ cup lemon juice
2 tablespoons grated orange peel	4 pounds breast of veal

Combine all ingredients except the veal in a roasting pan, to make a marinade. Trim all fat from veal and place in pan. Refrigerate ½ hour, turning once. Preheat broiler 350° for 15 minutes, lower flame to 325° and place meat with curved side on bottom (like a boat), at furthest point from heat. Broil 20 minutes. When crusty and well done, turn. Baste with marinade and broil another 20 minutes. Total cooking time: 40 to 50 minutes. You can also do this on your outside barbecue.

Ten ounces of veal is a dinner meat serving.

CHINESE   BUTTERFLY SHRIMP

8 ounces shrimp in shell	Paprika
Cold water	Pinch garlic powder
Salt	⅓ cup dry powdered skim milk
Pepper	

Remove shell from shrimp but leave on the tail. Wash and devein, then cut shrimp open and spread flat to make a butterfly shape. Moisten shrimp with cold water and sprinkle with salt, pepper, paprika and a pinch of garlic powder. Set aside. Put ⅓ cup of powdered skim milk into a small bowl and dip each shrimp into it to coat it. Broil close to the flame for 5 minutes on each side.

This is a dinner seafood serving and a glass of milk.

CHINESE   **CHICKEN CHOW MEIN**

6 ounces cooked chicken, shredded	Celery stalks, in chunks
1 can bean sprouts	1 chicken bouillon cube dissolved in a cup of hot water
2 ounces bamboo shoots	
1 can mushrooms	1 Chinese cabbage, sliced
2 ounces water chestnuts	Garlic powder

Shred the cooked chicken and set aside. Cook celery in the chicken bouillon to soften and set aside. Mix and heat the bean sprouts, bamboo shoots, mushrooms, water chestnuts, cooked celery chunks and Chinese cabbage. Season to taste with garlic powder and drain well. Add shredded chicken. Serve with Chinese mustard on the side.

This recipe is one dinner serving and one dinner vegetable and it makes a tremendous platter!

CHINESE   **FRIED CHICKEN**

6 ounces cooked chicken, diced	3 tablespoons soy sauce
¼ teaspoon salt	DW fried bean sprouts
¼ teaspoon white pepper	2 ounces scallion chopped fine

Heat Teflon pan. Add the chicken, salt and white pepper. Raise flame and brown chicken, stirring until golden. Add soy sauce, reduce flame and cook 2 minutes longer. Serve on bed of fried bean sprouts with chopped scallions sprinkled on top.

This equals a dinner meat serving and two ounces of a dinner vegetable.

CHINESE   **LOBSTER DELIGHT**

1-pound lobster	⅛ teaspoon black pepper
8 scallions (with greens), diced fine	⅛ teaspoon basil
2 green peppers, diced	½ pound green peas
1 clove garlic, minced	1 can bean sprouts
⅛ teaspoon paprika	1 can mushrooms
	4 ounces soy sauce

Bring one quart of water to a boil. Add the lobster. When shell turns red, lobster meat is tender. Drain liquid, let lobster cool, then remove meat and cut into chunks. Sauté the scallions in a Teflon pot. Add the diced green peppers, garlic, paprika, black pepper, soy sauce and basil, stirring well. Cover and simmer 10 minutes or until pepper is tender. Add the green peas, and cover and simmer 5 minutes more. Add the lobster chunks, mix and continue simmering 10 minutes. Mix and heat the bean sprouts and mushrooms, drain them well and make into a bed on the serving platter. Top them with the lobster and serve.

The lobster is a dinner seafood serving. Four ounces of the scallion and green peas combined are a dinner vegetable. The other vegetables are unlimited.

CHINESE   PEPPER STEAK

1 pound flank steak	¼ cup cold water
½ clove garlic, diced fine or ½ teaspoon garlic powder	4 tablespoons soy sauce
	½ teaspoon liquid non-sugar sweetener
½ teaspoon salt	3 scallions, cut in 1 ½ inch pieces
½ teaspoon white pepper	
1 teaspoon mashed green ginger root (optional)	1 can whole mushrooms, drained
6 green peppers, cut in ½ inch strips	1 scallion (including greens), minced

Slice steak diagonally into short pieces, across the grain. Put meat into Teflon pan together with the garlic, salt, pepper and ginger root. Cover and cook until the beef is almost done (just 1 or 2 minutes). Remove the beef to a plate and to the Teflon pan add the green pepper strips, water, soy sauce, sweetener and scallion strips. Cook until pepper is tender. Shut flame and let cool. Refrigerate. Skim off the fat and wash the Teflon pan to remove all fat. Now return everything to the pan including the beef and the mushrooms, and heat and serve. On the serving platter, top everything with the minced scallion.

Six ounces is a beef dinner serving and half the scallions are two ounces of dinner vegetable.

CHINESE   "ROAST PORK"

½ teaspoon garlic powder	¼ cup liquid non-sugar sweetener
½ cup soy sauce	2 pounds shoulder of veal

Combine the soy sauce and sweetener. Cut veal into 3 lengthwise pieces and place in shallow dish, covering with the sauce. Marinate in refrigerator 1 hour, turning 2 or 3 times. Preheat broiler 15 minutes at 350°, lay meat on rack in broiler about 6 to 8 inches below flame, lower flame to 325° and broil 30 minutes (until one side is crisp). Turn, add marinating sauce and continue broiling to crisp other side. Total cooking time: 1-1 ½ hours.

You can also do this on a rotisserie. Buy a rolled shoulder of veal and marinate it whole in the sauce, turning as needed. Only the outside will have the marinade flavor. When you spit it, sprinkle lightly with more garlic powder and paprika and let it barbecue 1 hour if roll is thin, or 1 ½ hours if thick. Slice thin and serve. Equally good hot or cold! Serve with pimientos as a side dish.

Six ounces equals one dinner meat serving.

CHINESE   **LOBSTER LO-MEIN**

6 ounces boiled lobster meat (use frozen lobster)	**Bamboo shoots**
	Cooked Chinese pea pods, or green peas
3 to 4 onions, sliced	**Kikkoman soy sauce or**
Water chestnuts	**dash salt and pepper**

Boil frozen lobster according to directions on the box and set aside. In a Teflon pan let the onion slices simmer, covered, 10 minutes. Remove cover and raise the flame to brown the onion. Add the water chestnuts, bamboo shoots and cooked Chinese pea pods or green peas, mixing well. Let simmer, covered, for 5 minutes. Weigh off 4 ounces and put these in a saucepan. Add six ounces of boiled lobster chunks and soy sauce to taste, or salt and pepper. Serve with Chinese mustard.

This equals a seafood dinner serving and one dinner vegetable.

CHINESE   **SHRIMP CHOW MEIN**

6 ounces cooked shrimp	**2 ounces scallion, diced**
1 can bean sprouts	**1 can mushrooms**
2 ounces combined of bamboo shoots and water chestnuts	**1 Chinese cabbage, sliced**
	Dash garlic powder

Heat all the ingredients together, except the shrimp. Add those toward the end. Drain well. Add garlic powder and mix. Serve with a side dish of Chinese mustard.

This is a dinner seafood serving and one dinner vegetable.

SUB GUM CHOW MEIN

6 ounces cooked chicken (or turkey white meat)

1 ½ ounces water chestnuts, drained

1 ½ ounces bamboo shoots

1 stalk celery, diced fine

1 ounce scallions (with greens), diced

2 stalks Chinese cabbage, sliced thin

1 can mushrooms, drained

2 green peppers, diced fine

½ can French-style string beans

¼ teaspoon white pepper

1 teaspoon liquid non-sugar sweetener

1 chicken bouillon cube dissolved in 1 cup hot water

2 tablespoons soy sauce DW rice Chinese mustard

Combine all ingredients but the last three in a Teflon pan and mix well. Cover, bring to boil, stir and add soy sauce. Reduce flame and simmer, covered, until vegetables are tender. Serve over DW rice, with Chinese mustard.

This equals a dinner serving and a dinner vegetable.

For variations, try this with shrimp or lobster instead of poultry.

SOUPS, SIDE DISHES AND SNACKS

CHINESE **VEGETABLE SOUP**
(Unlimited)

1 chicken bouillon cube

1 cup boiling water

½ can French-style string beans, drained

½ can bean sprouts, drained

½ can mushrooms, drained

2 stalks Chinese cabbage, shredded

Dissolve chicken bouillon cube in the boiling water. Add the string beans, bean sprouts, mushrooms and Chinese cabbage. Heat everything together and serve piping hot. For a different sensational flavor add ½ teaspoon of DW Mild Chinese Mustard to the soup.

CHINESE **ANYTIME CHOP SUEY**
(Unlimited)

½ green cabbage	½ pound cooked mush-
1 green pepper, sliced	rooms, or 1 can,
1 red pepper, sliced	drained
⅓ cup tomato juice	2 stalks celery, diced
2 to 3 drops non-sugar	1 can French-style string
liquid sweetener	beans, drained
Salt and pepper to taste	1 can bean sprouts,
1 clove garlic, minced or	drained
½ teaspoon garlic	Chinese mustard
powder	

Shred cabbage and then cook it together with the peppers, tomato juice, sweetener, seasonings and garlic for 15 to 20 minutes. When cabbage is soft, add all the rest of the ingredients to heat them. Drain all liquid and serve with hot Chinese mustard.

Delicious, satisfying and absolutely unlimited!

CHINESE   CABBAGE AND MUSHROOMS
(Unlimited)

1 pound fresh mushrooms	⅓ teaspoon pepper
1 small Chinese cabbage	⅓ teaspoon salt
in chunks	

Wash mushrooms thoroughly, separate the stems and put them into a Teflon pan. Add the cabbage, pepper and salt. Cover and cook on a low flame—do not add liquid. Let simmer, stirring until all water from mushrooms evaporates. Then test cabbage. If tender, it is ready to eat. If cabbage is not tender, add 2 tablespoons of water and continue cooking.

CHINESE   FRIED BEAN SPROUTS
(Unlimited)

1 can bean sprouts	Parsley
Choy brand	2 tablespoons tomato
Paprika	juice
Garlic powder	

Drain bean sprouts well. Spread out on Teflon pan and sprinkle with paprika, garlic powder, a drop of parsley flakes and the tomato juice. Mix together. Cover and simmer about 2 minutes, just so that sprouts pick up flavor. Remove cover, raise flame and brown, stirring with wooden spatula.

(This will burn your Teflon pan, but I keep one just for browning—it's *burnt*, but that's its purpose! I don't worry about scrubbing off the browned bottom.)

CHINESE GREEN BEANS

1 chicken bouillon cube	2 tablespoons soy sauce
¼ cup hot water	1 pound fresh string
2 cloves garlic, diced fine	beans, cut up
4 ounces onion (or 1 medium onion) diced	

Dissolve 1 chicken bouillon cube in ¼ cup water. Place the garlic, onion and 1 tablespoon of the bouillon in a pan and cook to brown the onion. Add soy sauce and string beans. Cover and simmer 10 minutes or until string beans are tender. Add more bouillon if the liquid evaporates.

Four ounces equal one dinner vegetable.

CHINESE PEA PODS

4 ounces Chinese pea pods   Small amount of water

If you can find a store that sells Chinese pea pods (many supermarkets carry them frozen) use this recipe:

String the pods as you would string beans and if they are large, cut them into chunks; otherwise use whole ones. Cook 4 ounces—do not use salt—for 10 minutes or until tender. Serve.

This equals a dinner vegetable.

If you cannot find a store that sells these pods, use the excellent DW recipe that follows:

CHINESE YOUR OWN CHINESE PEA PODS

4 ounces fresh green peas   Pinch Salt
Water

If you can't buy Chinese pea pods, wash skin of fresh green peas well, and shell them. Cut skin open at the bottom and then cut into 1-inch slices. Cook together with the peas in your pressure cooker, or use a regular saucepan, cooking in just enough water to steam cook, until tender. Add salt to you taste.

This equals one dinner vegetable.

CHINESE RICE SALAD

1 can bean sprouts, well drained	½ cup radishes sliced thin
2 stalks celery sliced diagonally	2 ounces carrots, shredded coarsely
2 green peppers, cut into 1 inch strips	DW Rice
2 ounces scallions sliced very thin	2 tablespoons soy sauce
	1 tablespoon vinegar

Combine the bean sprouts, celery, green peppers, scallions, radish slices and carrots. Add DW rice. Mix well and refrigerate. Just before serving, add soy sauce and vinegar and toss lightly.

This recipe is a dinner vegetable.

CHINESE   **HOT CHINESE MUSTARD**
(Unlimited)

**Coleman's English
mustard or any dry
mustard powder**

To each teaspoon of powder add 2 tablespoons of water. Mix—that's it! The less water you use the stronger the mustard.

CHINESE   **MILD CHINESE MUSTARD**
(Unlimited)

**½ teaspoon dry powdered   2 tablespoons water
mustard**

Mix and serve.

CHINESE   **ORANGE SAUCE**

**1 orange   Dash salt
4 ounces unsweetened   3 tablespoons non-sugar
orange juice, fresh or   liquid sweetener
frozen**

Wash orange well and grate off skin, using a grater. Mix the grated rind with the orange juice and add the salt and sweetener. Boil 4 or 5 minutes. Segment the rest of the orange into very small sections, removing any skin and seeds and add to the boiled juice. You should have 1 cup of orange sauce. Use as a flavoring for fish, lamb chops, veal or chicken.

This recipe equals two fruits. Half a cup equals one fruit and a two-ounce side dish equals half a fruit.

CHINESE   **ORANGE SPROUTS**

**1 can bean sprouts,   ½ cup DW Orange Sauce
drained well**

Place drained sprouts in Teflon pan and brown well. Add the orange sauce, mix, heat and serve. A delicious side dish!

This equals one fruit.

DINNERS

HAWAIIAN BAKED HAWAIIAN FISH

Any fish you like, 8
ounces
½ cup water
1 tablespoon vinegar
1 teaspoon liquid non-
sugar sweetener
1 bay leaf, broken up

2 ounces onion, sliced
¼ teaspoon salt
¼ teaspoon black pepper
2 tablespoons parsley
2 lemons sliced thin

Combine the water, vinegar, sweetener and bay leaf in a baking pan. Add the onions and arrange the fish on them. Sprinkle salt, pepper and parsley over the fish. In 350° oven bake 20 minutes, until lightly browned. Serve with thin lemon slices as a garnish.

This is a dinner fish serving and two ounces of a dinner vegetable.

HAWAIIAN BEACHCOMBER'S SKEWER
SURPRISE
(Great for a beach picnic)

3 ounces dark meat of
roasted turkey
3 ounces frankfurters
½ fresh pineapple
⅓ cup No-Cal cherry
syrup

4 ounces small white
onions
1 pound fresh mushrooms,
or 1 can whole ones,
drained

At home: cut the turkey into 1 ½ inch chunks. Cut frankfurters into 1 ½ inch pieces. Peel and cut the pineapple into 1 ½ inch chunks and cook them in the cherry syrup until tender to a fork test (15 to 20 minutes). Reserve the cooking liquid.

At the beach: On the skewer arrange in order, pineapple, turkey, mushroom, onion, frankfurter, pineapple. Continue to alternate until the serving is complete. Brush on the leftover pineapple-cherry liquid. Grill over charcoal, or on your broiler if you're picnicing at home, until franks are well-done. Serve with a large tossed green salad that has lots of cucumber.

This recipe equals a dinner beef serving, a dinner vegetable and one fruit for the day.

HAWAIIAN **LAMB BARBECUE**

4 **pounds breast of lamb**	¾ **cup vinegar**
Dash paprika	¼ **cup soy sauce**
Dash garlic powder	¼ **cup lemon juice**
1 **chicken bouillon cube**	¼ **cup liquid**
½ **cup hot water**	**non-sugar sweetener**

With a sharp knife cut through the racks of lamb so they look like spare ribs. Trim all fat. Sprinkle with paprika and garlic powder and let stand ½ hour. Place the bouillon cube, hot water, vinegar, soy sauce, lemon juice and sweetener in a roasting pan and mix to dissolve the bouillon cube. Marinate the lamb racks in this mixture at least 1 hour. Roast in a 350° oven 1 ½ hours. Serve with hot Chinese mustard. These are also delicious served with ½ cup Dole's crushed pineapple.

10 ounces cooked lamb equal a dinner beef serving. The pineapple on the side is a fruit for the day.

HAWAIIAN **BEEF LUAU**

3 **pounds short ribs**	½ **cup vinegar**
Paprika	⅛ **cup soy sauce**
Garlic powder	⅛ **cup lemon juice**
1 **chicken bouillon cube**	⅛ **cup liquid**
½ **cup hot water**	**non-sugar sweetener**

Score the meat on both sides to absorb a marinating mixture and sprinkle it with paprika and garlic powder. Dissolve bouillon cube in the hot water and combine with the vinegar, soy sauce, lemon juice and sweetener. Marinate the beef in this sauce 2 hours. Prepare your outdoor barbecue and when the coals are gray, grill meat on 1 side. Brush the undone side lightly with marinade and broil. Grill as high from the flame as possible. Slice diagonally like London broil and serve immediately with hot Chinese mustard.

Six ounces is a dinner beef serving.

This is delicious with sliced unsweetened pineapple. Use a brand that is packed in its own juice. Marinate it in the sauce with the meat and grill it with the meat. Four slices of pineapple is a fruit for the day.

HAWAIIAN **ISLAND CHICKEN**

Barbecue Sauce (see	**Dash paprika**
Hawaiian Barbecued	**Chopped parsley**
Spare Ribs)	**Garlic powder**
2 **broilers, 3 pounds each**	

This is a marvelous way to use up refrigerated Hawaiian sauce left over from Barbecued Spare Ribs:

Skim off the fat and heat in a saucepan. Transfer to a roasting pan and let cool. Cut the broilers as for Southern fried chicken, and sprinkle with paprika, parsley and garlic powder. Let stand ½ hour, then place in the sauce and marinate 2 hours, turning every half hour. Roast in a 350° oven, in the sauce, 1 ½ hours. Remove chicken and discard sauce. The chicken can be frozen for party time and re-heated on your outside grill or under your oven broiler.

One-half chicken is a dinner serving.

HAWAIIAN LAMB ROAST

¾ of a leg of lamb
Salt
Pepper
Dash garlic powder
4 ounces onion, chopped
4 ounces orange juice
2 tablespoons prepared mustard
¾ teaspoon rosemary

Sprinkle the lamb lightly with salt, pepper, garlic powder. Preheat oven at 350° for 5 minutes, reduce to 325° and roast the lamb in a shallow roasting pan 30 to 35 minutes per pound, for medium doneness. Combine the onion, orange juice, prepared mustard and rosemary and baste the meat with this sauce during the last hour of cooking.

A six-ounce (sliced) portion is a one dinner beef serving. One cup of the sauce equals half a dinner vegetable and half a fruit for the day.

HAWAIIAN SWEET AND SOUR BEEF BALLS

1 cup unsweetened pineapple juice
1 tablespoon No-Cal cherry syrup
1 tablespoon Kikkoman soy sauce
2 chicken bouillon cubes
4 ounces carrots
½ pound asparagus, cut in two-inch pieces
3 green peppers, diced
1 pound crab apples diced (unpeeled)
1 can pineapple chunks, unsweetened
1 pound ground beef
⅓ cup ice water

Combine the juice, syrup and the soy sauce and heat in a large saucepan. Add the chicken bouillon cubes (stir to dissolve). Taste and add sweetener or water as you prefer. Cut carrots diagonally into ovals and add them to the sauce. Also add the asparagus, peppers, pineapple and set aside. Now combine the beef and ice water. Wet hands with cold water, then make tiny (1-inch) beef balls. Set aside. Bring the sauce to a quick boil and gently lower the beef balls over the other ingredients. Reduce flame, cover and simmer 1 ½ hours.

Six ounces of beef balls are a dinner beef serving. The carrots are a dinner vegetable. A half cup of apples and pineapple combined equal one fruit.

HAWAIIAN **LAMB AND PINEAPPLE BURGERS**

14-ounce can Dole's sliced pineapple (unsweetened)	½ teaspoon salt
	¼ teaspoon pepper
1 ½ pounds lamb, ground	½ teaspoon dried rosemary
4 ounces onion, diced	

Drain the pineapple, reserving the liquid. In a mixing bowl, combine the lamb, onion and seasonings, mixing well. Shape this mixture into thick patties and place them in a preheated broiler, 3 or 4 inches from the flame. Broil 6 to 8 minutes. Turn and place a slice of pineapple on top of each patty. Broil 6 minutes more. Serve.

Six ounces are a dinner beef serving. Four pineapple slices are one fruit for the day.

HAWAIIAN **OVEN BARBECUED CHICKEN BURGERS**

½ pound boned breast of chicken or 1 ¼ pounds chicken thighs	⅛ teaspoon terragon
	½ tablespoon lemon juice
1 tablespoon prepared mustard	

Buy boned chicken breasts, or bone them yourself. Salt both sides of chicken and arrange skin side up in a baking dish. Set aside. In a small bowl combine the mustard, terragon and lemon juice. Brush half of mixture on top of the chicken. Bake 15 to 20 minutes in a preheated 400° oven. When golden brown, turn and brush the other side with the sauce. Continue baking until second side is brown. The barbecue sauce makes this something truly special! Heat 4 ounces of mixed carrots and peas as a side dish, or serve with Chinese pea pods.

This recipe equals a dinner serving and the side dish is a dinner vegetable.

HAWAIIAN **SAVORY LAMB CHOPS**

2 shoulder, rib or loin   1 teaspoon paprika
   lamb chops ½ inch   1 clove garlic, minced
   thick, or 3 baby ones   ¼ teaspoon pepper
2 tablespoons water   1 teaspoon salt
1 tablespoon vinegar

Trim all visible fat. Broil the chops 5 minutes on each side, just to brown them and let fat drip off. Then place them in a Teflon pan, add all the rest of the ingredients and simmer about 30 minutes, or until all the liquid has evaporated and the pot is bone dry. Turn the chops once or twice so they absorb everything.

This is a dinner beef serving.

SIDE DISHES AND SNACKS

HAWAIIAN **ISLAND RELISH**
(Dinner only)

½ cup orange No-Cal   1 bunch carrots
   syrup   1 fresh pineapple
¼ cup cold water   Pinch cinnamon

Combine the orange syrup and water. Slice and cut the carrots and pineapple into small chunks. Cook them in the orange liquid until tender (about ½ hour). Remove from flame and let cool. Transfer to blender, add a pinch of cinnamon and blend into a relish consistency. Delicious hot or cold with veal, lamb, chicken or turkey.

One cup is a dinner vegetable and a fruit for the day.

You can also make this by substituting ½ glass of orange diet soda for the orange syrup. Or you can dilute a package of Pillsbury Funny Face powder with one quart of cold water, stir and use ½ cup for the relish. (Save the rest for a refreshing cold drink).

HAWAIIAN MARINATED CHINESE CABBAGE
(Unlimited)

1 teaspoon pickling spices   Chinese cabbage, cut
⅓ cup vinegar   in chunks
2 teaspoons non-sugar
   liquid sweetener

Combine the pickling spices, vinegar and sweetener and bring to a boil. Strain and pour over the Chinese cabbage. Let stand over night.

HAWAIIAN   STUFFED TOMATO SALAD

One tomato
**1 can baby green peas,
    drained**

Dash garlic powder
**1 tablespoon chopped or
    dehydrated parsley**

Halve the tomato and remove the center pulp carefully.
Chop the pulp and toss with the green peas. Add a drop of
garlic powder and parsley and stuff the mix into the tomato
shells. Broil far from flame, just until tomato is soft (10 to
15 minutes).

Four ounces is a dinner vegetable.

HAWAIIAN   TANGY FRUIT COCKTAIL

**4 ounces chilled
    buttermilk**

**4 ounces orange juice,
    unsweetened**

Combine, shake in a jar or cocktail shaker and drink up!
This is ½ glass of milk and one fruit for the day.

NORTH OF THE BORDER

NORTH OF THE BORDER

CANADIAN **CHERRY-PEAR PANCAKES**
(Breakfast only)

1 slice white bread
1 egg
2 capfuls No-Cal cherry
syrup

1 fresh pear
Dash cinnamon

Toast the bread and use blender to make bread crumbs. Set aside. Peel and slice the pear thinly. Combine the egg, cherry syrup, pear slices and cinnamon. Put them through the blender until pear is pureéd. Mix with the bread crumbs. Heat a Teflon pan and pour in this batter. Fry on medium flame, and when brown, turn and fry the other side.

The pear equals one fruit for the day.

CANADIAN ·TUNA PIE CASSEROLE
(Lunch only)

¾ package frozen spinach
1 can tuna fish (3 ¾
  ounces) drained
1 can sliced mushrooms,
  drained

1 tablespoon prepared
  mustard
Parsley
1 slice white bread

Cook spinach according to directions on the box and drain well. Combine it with the tuna fish, mushrooms and mustard, mixing thoroughly. Set aside. Cut crusts from the bread and reserve them. Roll out the center with a rolling pin or soda bottle and put the thinned slice in a small casserole or 4 inch pie plate. Cover with the tuna mixture and top the tuna with the strips of bread crust in a lattice-work design. Sprinkle with parsley. Bake in preheated 350° oven 15 to 20 minutes (until top browns and bubbles).

109

DINNERS

CANADIAN   SALMON DUMPLINGS OR CROQUETTES

¼ cup tomato juice
⅓ cup dry powdered skim milk
7 ounces canned salmon, drained
½ green pepper, diced
2 ounces onion, diced
1 stalk celery, diced

Dash black pepper
½ teaspoon parsley
Dash garlic powder
Dash salt
2 ounces cherry (or sliced) tomatoes
Parsley sprigs

Line the broiler with aluminum foil and moisten this with a few drops of tomato juice. Put the powdered milk into a medium sized bowl. In another bowl, mash the salmon fine and then combine it with the onion, green pepper, celery, black pepper, parsley flakes and garlic powder, mixing well. Add salt if you like. Wet both hands with cold water and roll salmon mixture in your palms into small (1 inch) balls. Dip each ball into the powdered milk to coat it, and set it on the aluminum foil. Pour a little tomato juice over each ball. Broil close to flame until brown, turn carefully, pour the rest of the tomato juice over all the croquettes and brown second side. Serve with the tomatoes and parsley.

This is a dinner fish serving, a dinner vegetable, a glass of milk and two ounces of tomato juice.

CANADIAN   TUNA CHOWDER

2 chicken bouillon cubes
2 cups hot water
¼ cup tomato juice
1 can tuna (6 ounces), drained
1 green pepper, chopped
1 can sliced mushrooms, drained

2 ounces canned peas and carrots
2 ounces onion, sliced
Dash Tabasco sauce
Dash black pepper

Dissolve the bouillon cubes in the hot water right in the saucepan. Flake the tuna meat with a fork; add flakes to the saucepan together with all the other ingredients, and stir. Simmer 10 minutes.

This recipe is a dinner fish serving, a dinner vegetable and two ounces of tomato juice for the day.

SIDE DISHES AND SNACKS

CANADIAN   FRENCH FRIED FLOWERETTES

1 fresh cauliflower, or 1 box frozen	Salt and pepper to taste

Break cauliflower into flowerettes. Cook in water until tender. Drain and brown on broiler, alone or along with any meat. Season with salt and pepper. Serve.

CANADIAN   MOLDED APPLE CIDER SALAD

2 tablespoons lemon juice	1 ½ cups hot cider
2 tablespoons water	½ cup red apples (diced but not peeled)
1 tablespoon gelatine (unflavored)	
3 tablespoons No-Cal cherry syrup	½ cup celery, diced Lettuce

Combine the lemon juice and water and soften the gelatine in this mixture. Add the sweetener and softened gelatine to 1 ½ cups hot cider and stir until completely dissolved. Chill in refrigerator until it begins to thicken. Meanwhile, dice the unpeeled red apples and the celery. Add this to the thickened gelatine and pour into one-cup molds. Chill thoroughly in refrigerator. Serve on a wedge of lettuce.

Each cup equals one fruit.

CANADIAN   SPINACH SUMMER SALAD
(Unlimited)

Raw spinach leaves	1 red pepper, in strips
Romaine lettuce	1 green pepper, in strips
Iceberg lettuce	6 red radishes, sliced
Boston lettuce	2 tablespoons garlic powder
Watercress	
Cucumber, sliced	Paprika
Summer squash, washed well and sliced thin	Parsley
Chinese cabbage leaves, diced fine	Lemon wedges

Wash the spinach leaves well and break them into bite-size pieces. Wash and tear the lettuce and watercress. Add the other salad ingredients and let them drain in a collander. Moisten a large wooden salad bowl with 2 or 3 drops of water and then rub garlic powder into the bowl well. Add all salad vegetables and toss thoroughly. Top with a dash of paprika, some parsley and a generous squeeze of lemon.

111

SOME LATIN PLEASURES

SOME LATIN PLEASURES

LATIN AMERICAN   **ARROZ CON POLLO # 1**

Broiler or fryer (2 ½
pounds)
Pepper
Paprika
Salt
DW rice (two portions)
1 chicken bouillon cube
dissolved in 1 cup hot
tomato juice

¼ teaspoon oregano
¼ cup parsley flakes
1 can sliced mushrooms,
drained
1 ounce onion, diced fine
1 bay leaf

Cut broiler as for frying and sprinkle generously with pepper, paprika and salt. Place the chicken skin side down in a Teflon pan and turn to brown it well. Add the bouillon-tomato mixture and oregano and bring to a boil. Cover, lower flame and cook on very small flame until chicken is tender and almost all broth is absorbed. During the last 5 minutes, stir in the parsley flakes, mushrooms, onion, bay leaf and DW rice. Cover and cook another 10 minutes, making sure the chicken is well done (allow up to 1 hour of total cooking time). Refrigerate. Skim off fat, then reheat and serve.

Half the chicken is one dinner portion, one ounce of a dinner vegetable and 8 ounces of tomato juice for the day.

LATIN AMERICAN   **ARROZ CON POLLO # 2**

1 broiler (2 ½ pounds) cut
into serving pieces
Salt
Pepper
Paprika
4 ounces onion, chopped
1 clove garlic, diced fine
4 ounces fresh tomatoes,
sliced

2 large red or green
peppers, in strips
½ teaspoon salt
2 cans bean sprouts,
drained well
Pinch saffron, or
turmeric (or yellow
vegetable coloring)

112

Season the chicken with salt, pepper and paprika and place in a Teflon pan with onion and garlic. Brown chicken well on a high flame. Transfer everything to a casserole dish. Add the tomatoes, peppers and salt. Chop the bean sprouts to rice size, mix with saffron or yellow coloring, and add it to the casserole. Cover, or use foil to seal and bake in 350° oven 1 hour.

Half the chicken and half the sauce are a dinner serving and a dinner vegetable.

LATIN AMERICAN   CHILI CON CARNE # 1
(A beef dish)

8 ounces chopped beef	2 green peppers
¼ cup cold water	4 ounces onion, sliced
Dash parsley flakes	1 can mushrooms, drained
¼ cup tomato juice	Dash chili, to taste
3 stalks celery, diced	

In a bowl, mix the beef, water and parsley flakes, and make into meatballs, the size of a nickel. Set aside. Sauté all the vegetables in the tomato juice, adding a dash of chili powder, until vegetables are tender (about 10 minutes). Add the meatballs to this simmering sauce and continue to cook until meat is done. Let cool, refrigerate, then skim fat that has congealed on top. Reheat to serve.

This is a dinner beef serving, one dinner vegetable and two ounces of tomato juice.

LATIN AMERICAN   CHILE CON CARNE # 2
(A veal dish)

½ pound veal, ground	¼ teaspoon salt
4 ounces onion, diced	1 teaspoon chile powder
1 green pepper, diced	(or two, according to
1 clove garlic, minced	taste)
(or ½ teaspoon garlic	1 cup tomato juice
powder)	

In a Teflon pan, brown the ground veal. Add the onion, green pepper and garlic. When the onions are browned, remove everything, drain off all the fat and wash the pan. Return food to pan, replace on burner and stir in the tomato juice, salt and chile powder. Taste. Add chile powder if you like it more piquant, but cautiously—this is a hot spice! Simmer, uncovered, for 15 minutes. Add one can of drained bean sprouts and, if you like, a can of drained mushrooms.

This is a dinner meat serving, one dinner vegetable, and eight-ounces of tomato juice for the day.

4 ounces lobster, shrimp and mussels, combined

1 peppercorn

1 clove garlic, diced fine

⅛ teaspoon oregano
Dash salt

¼ teaspoon vinegar

2 ounces raw chicken cut in strips

1 green pepper, chopped

⅛ teaspoon ground coriander

3 tablespoons tomato juice

1 serving DW rice

2 tablespoons parsley

1 cup boiling water

⅛ teaspoon saffron or yellow food coloring

2 ounces canned peas, drained

2 pimientos, in strips

Remove lobster meat from shell. Scrub mussels well. Shell, wash and devein the shrimp. Mash the peppercorn and garlic and combine them with the oregano, salt and vinegar. Rub the raw chicken with this mixture. Brown chicken lightly in a preheated Teflon pan and add the green pepper, coriander. Cover' and cook 10 minutes on a very low flame. Add the tomato juice, DW rice and parsley and cook 5 minutes more. Add the boiling water, saffron or yellow food coloring, and the shrimp, mixing everything well. Cook, covered, over high flame until all liquid is absorbed (about 20 minutes). Now add the lobster meat, peas and pimientos. Cover and cook 5 minutes longer. In a separate pot, steam the mussels in a little water until the shells open. Transfer everything to a deep serving platter, garnishing with the mussels.

This recipe is a dinner seafood serving and one dinner vegetable.

AS AMERICAN AS . . .

AS AMERICAN AS . . .

BREAKFASTS

AMERICAN   **COTTAGE CHEESE
GRIDDLE CAKES**
(Breakfast only)

2 ounces cottage cheese
  White of 1 egg
¼ cup skim milk
2 tablespoons No-Cal
  sour cherry syrup (or
  other flavor you like)

1 slice white bread
  Dash cinnamon or
  nutmeg

Mix the cottage cheese, egg white and skim milk until smooth. Add the No-Cal syrup. Line broiler pan with foil and toast one side of the bread on it. Turn bread and top with cheese mixture. Broil 3 inches from flame until bubbly and brown. Sprinkle with a dash of cinnamon or nutmeg.

This recipe equals ¼ cup milk.

AMERICAN   **COUNTRY BREAKFAST**

1 hard boiled egg, sliced
1 box frozen cauliflower
1 small can mushrooms

1 slice white bread
  Parsley flakes

Hardboil one egg and slice it. Cook the cauliflower according to box directions, and then overcook and drain. Drain the liquid from the can of mushrooms, and purée cauliflower in blender with the mushroom liquid. Heat the mushrooms in this sauce. Toast the bread, place the sliced egg on it and top with the mushrooms and sauce. Garnish with parsley flakes.

AMERICAN   **EGG GRIDDLE CAKES**
(Breakfast only)

1 slice enriched white bread
1 cup cooked summer
  squash, drained
1 tablespoon orange No-
  Cal syrup

1 egg, beaten
⅓ cup skim milk
  Pinch salt
  Cinnamon

Toast the bread and put it through the blender for bread crumbs. In a bowl, mix the cooked summer squash and the syrup. Add the beaten egg, milk and salt. Mix lightly, adding the bread crumbs. Pour into a hot Teflon pan. Brown and turn carefully to brown on other side. Sprinkle lightly with cinnamon and serve.

This recipe equals 1/3 cup milk.

AMERICAN **GEORGE WASHINGTON PANCAKES**

1 **slice white bread**	1 **tablespoon cherry No-Cal syrup**
½ **cup skim milk**	½ **cup fresh or frozen rasp-berries or strawberries**
1 **egg**	

Toast the slice of white bread and put through blender to make crumbs. Mix crumbs with the skim milk, egg, cherry No-Cal syrup (or any flavor you like), raspberries or strawberries. Preheat Teflon frypan, pour in batter and fry one side. Carefully turn to fry other side.

This recipe equals one-half glass of milk and one fruit.

AMERICAN **LEMON MUSHROOMS ON TOAST**
(For breakfast or lunch)

1 **clove of garlic**	1 **pound fresh mushrooms**
⅛ **teaspoon (optional) imita-tion butter flavoring, or to taste**	1 **teaspoon lemon juice**
	Dash salt
	Chopped parsley

Peel garlic and rub a skillet with it. Add the butter flavoring. Heat, adding the fresh mushrooms and stirring to coat them with butter flavoring. Add lemon juice and toss lightly. Cover skillet and simmer 5 minutes. To serve, garnish with chopped parsley.

Delicious for lunch on a slice of toast.

For breakfast: add it to a Teflon scrambled egg. Or make a bull's eye egg on toast, topped with lemon mushrooms.

LUNCHES

AMERICAN **NEW ENGLAND SHRIMP WITH MUSHROOMS**
(Lunch only)

1 **pound fresh mushrooms**	½ **tablespoon parsley flakes**
⅛ **teaspoon (optional) imita-tion butter flavoring**	1 **slice white bread**
4 **ounces cooked shrimp**	**Dash paprika**

116

Wash mushrooms. Break off stems of mushrooms and slice them (keep caps whole). Simmer the slices and caps in a covered Teflon pan, without water, until tender (5 to 10 minutes). Drain any liquid. Coat a baking dish with just a few drops of the butter flavoring. Add the cooked shrimp, mushrooms, parsley flakes. Sprinkle paprika on top to add color. Toast the slice of bread and put it through the blender to make crumbs. Mix them with the rest of the butter flavoring. Sprinkle them over the shrimp and mushrooms. Bake in 350° oven 15 to 20 minutes or until brown. Serve with a large tossed salad.

AMERICAN SOUTHERN SALMON BAKE

1 slice bread	Dash lemon
1 stalk celery,	juice
diced fine	2 slices red pepper
1 green pepper, diced	Paprika
3 and ¾-ounce can of	
salmon (or tuna),	
drained	

Toast bread and put through blender to make crumbs. Put celery, green pepper and fish through the blender for 2 minutes. Combine this mixture with the crumbs and lemon juice. Shape some aluminum foil into a boat shape by turning up the ends and fill the "mold" with the fish mixture, using a fork to shape the boat and to make lengthwise ridges across the top. Cover with two slices of red pepper and sprinkle entire top with paprika. Bake in a 350° oven 15 minutes, or place under the broiler, *far from the flame,* until it crusts on top. For variation, try this with canned tuna.

This equals one lunch, including one slice of bread.

AMERICAN STUFFED GRAPEFRUIT
(A perfect luncheon dish)

½ grapefruit	Radish roses, or sliced
3 ¾ ounces tuna	radishes
Parsley	Lettuce leaves
Paprika	Fresh mushrooms
Garlic powder	Cauliflowerettes
2 tablespoons buttermilk	

With a sharp knife cut a sawtooth edge around the half grapefruit. Use a grapefruit knife to scoop out the fruit sections. Make a clean grapefruit shell and set aside. Flake the tuna with a fork and combine it with a dash of parsley, the buttermilk, a bit of paprika and garlic powder to taste. Mix well to cream. Place half the grapefruit sections on the bottom of the fruit shell and top them with a pyramid of the tuna mixture, leaving some space all around the tuna in the shell. Circle the tuna with the rest of the grapefruit sections and with the radishes. Place the shell on crisp lettuce, with fresh mushrooms and cauliflowerettes to munch on.

A half shell is a lunch fish serving and a fruit for the day.

DINNERS

AMERICAN   AMERICAN FISH FRY

8 **ounces fish fillets**
(flounder, shrimp
or codfish)
2 **tablespoons skim milk**
¼ **teaspoon salt**
Paprika

Parsley flakes
⅓ **cup dry skim milk**
powder
Sprigs of parsley
Lemon wedges

Wash the fish. In a bowl combine the skim liquid milk with the salt, a dash of paprika and a sprinkling of parsley, mixing well. Spread the dry milk powder out on a sheet of wax paper or foil. Dip fish into the liquid mixture, then roll it in the powdered milk. Moisten your broiler pan with a few drops of liquid milk and arrange the coated fish in it. Broil under high heat, just 2 inches from the flame 3 to 5 minutes on each side, or until brown and crisp. Serve, garnished with parsley sprigs and lemon wedges.

This recipe equals one dinner fish serving, and one glass plus two tablespoons of milk.

AMERICAN   BARBECUED BREAST OF
LAMB

3 **or 4 pounds of lamb**
Paprika
Parsley flakes
1 **chicken bouillon cube**
dissolved in 1 cup
boiling water
1 **cup vinegar**

¼ **cup soy sauce**
¼ **cup lemon juice**
1 **clove garlic, diced fine**
¼ **cup liquid non-sugar**
sweetener
Butternut squash
Cinnamon

Trim fat from lamb. Rub lamb with paprika and parsley and set aside. To make the marinade, combine the chicken bouillon, vinegar, soy sauce, lemon juice, garlic and sweetener. Marinate the lamb in this sauce 2 to 3 hours. Grill on charcoal, far from flame, ½ hour or to your desired doneness.

118

Ten ounces of lamb cooked equal a dinner beef serving.

Marvelous with grilled butternut squash: Cut the squash in half, sprinkle with cinnamon and sweetener, wrap it in foil and broil at the same time as the lamb. For the final touch, add a spinach summer salad.

The butternut squash is a dinner vegetable.

AMERICAN   BARBECUED BROOK TROUT

10 ounces raw trout   **Garlic powder**
   Paprika   **Parsley**

Have the fish dealer clean and trim the head, tail, fins and scales. Sprinkle trout with paprika, garlic powder and parsley, inside and outside. Grill fish over charcoal 5 minutes, turn carefully and grill the second side for 5 minutes. Serve! For variation, try this recipe with a small flounder or bluefish.

This equals a fish dinner serving.

AMERICAN   BARBECUED ROCK CORNISH HEN

1 frozen Rock Cornish   **Paprika**
   Hen (1 ¼ pounds)   **Parsley flakes**
   Garlic powder

Thaw the hen, wash it well and rub with garlic powder, paprika and parsley, outside and inside. Place it on a spit, securing it well with the prongs. Set rotisserie for high heat and roast 1 hour. Serve with a tossed salad.

One hen is a dinner meat serving.

AMERICAN   BARBECUED VEAL CHOPS

2 veal chops (loin or rib),   **Zucchini, in 3 inch**
   each ½ inch thick   **chunks**
   Garlic powder   **Fresh mushrooms**
   Paprika

Sprinkle the veal with garlic powder and parsley and place on grill, alongside a skewer of zucchini and fresh mushrooms. Grill 10 to 15 minutes on each side until well done. Serve!

This is a dinner meat serving and the four ounces of zucchini are a dinner vegetable.

119

AMERICAN FRANKFURTER SURPRISE DINNER

2 tablespoons prepared mustard	½ pound franks
¼ cup liquid non-sugar sweetener	1 medium tart apple, cored, quartered

In heavy skillet mix well the mustard and sweetener. Slash each frank crosswise three times but do not cut through. Add franks and apple to skillet. Simmer covered 15 minutes, turning once to glaze everything, until apples are tender and heated through. The last five minutes open a can of sauerkraut. Drain* and add sauerkraut to skillet, heating with other ingredients.

This recipe equals a dinner beef serving and one fruit.

*Reserve juice for German apple dish (see index).

AMERICAN   LOBSTER FLORIDA

2 ounces onion, diced	Dash black pepper
2 green peppers, chopped	⅛ teaspoon basil
1 clove garlic, minced	6 ounces lobster chunks
⅛ teaspoon paprika	

Sauté the onion, pepper, garlic, paprika and basil in an uncovered Teflon skillet, stirring well. Cover pan and let simmer 10 to 15 minutes or until peppers are tender. Add the lobster, mixing all together well. Cover again and simmer 10 minutes more. Serve with cooked cauliflower, two ounces of sliced beets and a green salad.

This equals one dinner seafood serving and half a dinner vegetable. The sliced beets would complete your dinner vegetable.

AMERICAN   LOBSTER MOUSSE

6 ounces cooked lobster meat	2 ounces onion, grated
1 tablespoon gelatine	Salt
¼ cup cold water	Pepper, fresh-ground
3 tablespoons lemon juice	Lettuce
¼ teaspoon liquid non-sugar sweetener	½ cucumber, sliced
1 cup celery, chopped	2 ounces tomato, sliced
	Watercress

Chop the lobster meat very fine and set aside. Soften the gelatine in the cold water, then heat and stir to dissolve. Add the lemon juice, sweetener, celery, onion and lobster meat. Salt and sprinkle with fresh-ground pepper to taste. Mix thoroughly and transfer to individual molds (those little fish molds are perfect for this). Chill in refrigerator until firm. To serve, turn the mousse out over a bed of crisp lettuce. Garnish with cucumber, watercress and tomato.

This is a dinner fish serving and a dinner vegetable.

AMERICAN   NEW ENGLAND
          CREAMED SCALLOPS

8 ounces fresh or frozen scallops

2 tablespoons DW Zingy Ketchup

1 cucumber, peeled

⅓ cup skim milk

1 scallion (with greens), diced fine

Salt and pepper

2 ounces roasted pimiento, (sold in jars), diced

Cut cucumber lengthwise into thin strips, then quarter each strip. Thaw the scallops if frozen and wash well under cold running water. Pat dry and cut scallops crosswise in rounds. Cook scallops in covered Teflon pan on small flame about 3 minutes. Remove cover, raise flame and brown until golden (3 minutes). Add the scallions and cucumbers and top them with the pimiento. Simmer covered another 3 minutes. Add DW Zingy Ketchup and milk. Continue cooking, stirring, until boiling begins. Serve. Season with salt and pepper at table.

This equals one dinner seafood serving and 1/3 glass of milk for the day.

AMERICAN   PINEAPPLE SCALLOPS
            KABOB DINNER

½ cup Dole's Pineapple chunks (packed without sugar), plus the can liquid

½ pound scallops

½ pound mushrooms

1 clove garlic, diced fine

2 green peppers, in strips

½ teaspoon parsley

2 ounces onion rings

½ teaspoon paprika

2 ounces tomato, sliced thick

Combine the pineapple juice, garlic, parsley and paprika. Add the scallops and mix thoroughly. Let scallops marinate ½ hour, then alternate tightly on a skewer: a scallop, pineapple chunk, mushroom, pepper, onion slice, tomato slice. Grill 10 minutes, turning to brown all sides. Serve with salad of all greens.

This is a dinner fish serving, a dinner vegetable and one fruit for the day.

AMERICAN   ROAST "PORK"
                      DINNER

1 teaspoon salt
½ teaspoon sage
½ teaspoon thyme
½ teaspoon black pepper
1 teaspoon whole cloves
1 ½ teaspoons whole allspice
1 bay leaf, crumbled
1 tablespoon slivered
   lemon rind

2 teaspoons lemon juice
2 bouillon cubes dissolved
   in 2 cups hot water
4 or 5 pound rolled veal
   roast
½ cup slivered carrots and
   onions, mixed

Combine the first ten ingredients. Bring to a boil and then let this sauce cool. Place the veal roast in a roasting pan and pour the sauce over it. Marinate in refrigerator for 12 hours, turning a few times. Remove veal from marinade (reserve the liquid) and brown it rapidly in a heavy skillet. Return veal to roasting pan and the marinade, add the carrots and onions and bake 2 hours, covered, in preheated 350° oven. Serve with the sauce. I like to roast this ahead of time and chill the gravy to remove any fat. Then I reheat to serve over veal slices. I offer it with pimiento or pickled red peppers on the side.

Six ounces cooked meat equals one dinner portion.

AMERICAN   SHAD (OR TUNA) ROE

½ pound fresh roe of shad
   (or tuna)
1 glass water

Dash salt
1 ounce sweet onion,
   diced fine

In fresh fishmarket buy ½ pound of roe from tuna, shad or any fish that contains roe. Bring water in saucepan to a boil, then gently add the roe. Simmer until roe turns red (20 to 30 minutes). Remove, drain, sprinkle with salt and the onion. Serve with tossed green salad and hot vegetables.

This is a dinner seafood serving and one ounce of a dinner vegetable.

AMERICAN **SHRIMP CREOLE**
(**Exotic and fast**)

8 ounces shrimp, shelled, cleaned and deveined	2 stalks Chinese cabbage, shredded, or a few leaves regular cabbage, shredded
½ can bean sprouts, drained	
8 ounce can mushrooms, drained	1 green pepper, diced
4 ounces French-style string beans, canned or frozen	4 ounces tomato juice, seasoned to taste with dash of pepper, basil, oregano, chile powder

Stew all vegetables in the seasoned tomato juice 5 minutes. Add the shrimp and simmer until shrimp is hot and the pepper and cabbage are tender (15 to 20 minutes). Serve!

This recipe equals one dinner fish serving and half a cup tomato juice. For a lunch portion, use four ounces of shrimp.

AMERICAN **SHRIMP OR LOBSTER DELAWARE**

2 ounces onion, chopped	½ teaspoon garlic powder
2 green peppers, diced	⅛ teaspoon basil
⅛ teaspoon paprika	2 ounces fresh tomatoes, sliced
½ teaspoon salt (optional)	
⅛ teaspoon black pepper	10 ounces shrimp

Sauté the onion in uncovered Teflon pan. Add the diced green peppers and season with paprika, salt, black pepper, garlic powder and basil, stirring well. Cover and simmer 10 minutes or until peppers are tender. Add the tomatoes, cover and simmer 5 minutes more. Add shrimp or lobster, mixing well. Cover and simmer another 10 minutes. Serve.

This equals one dinner seafood serving and one dinner vegetable.

AMERICAN **STUFFED BREAST OF VEAL**

1 breast of veal (2 pounds)	1 can diced mushrooms, drained
1 package frozen cauliflower, cooked and drained, mashed fine	1 chicken bouillon cube dissolved in ½ cup hot water
1 can French-style string beans, drained and chopped	

Have butcher trim and make a pocket in the veal. To make stuffing: Combine all the rest of the ingredients, mixing well,

123

and stuff this into the veal pocket. Sew opening with white thread. Sprinkle paprika, garlic powder, parsley over veal. Place in roasting pan bone side down, add 1 cup water, lower oven heat from preheated 375° to 350°, and roast veal 1 hour (baste every 15 to 20 minutes with liquid, adding water if needed). Then turn veal and cook ½ hour longer. Transfer to serving platter. Remove sewing thread and slice through racks into 3 equal portions.

Each slice is a dinner meat serving.

AMERICAN VEAL CHOPS WITH BROWN SAUCE

1 cup hot water	1 teaspoon soy sauce
2 chicken bouillon cubes	2 veal chops, cut ½-inch
½ teaspoon oregano	thick

Combine the hot water, bouillon cubes, oregano and soy sauce. Pour sauce over the veal chops and bake in 350° oven until veal is tender (about 45 minutes).

This recipe equals one dinner meat serving.

SOUPS, SIDE DISHES, SNACKS AND SAUCES

AMERICAN CREAMED MUSHROOM SOUP
(Anytime soup)

1 can asparagus, juice included	Dash paprika
	¼ teaspoon parsley
⅓ cup powdered dry skim milk	1 can mushrooms, drained

Purée the asparagus, juice included, in the blender with all the other ingredients except mushrooms. Put into saucepan, add mushrooms, heat, serve with salt and pepper to taste.

This recipe equals one glass of milk.

AMERICAN CRANBERRY SALAD

2 cups raw cranberries, blended	1 ½ cups hot water
2 ounces orange juice	1 tablespoon non-sugar liquid sweetener
1 envelope unflavored gelatine	1 teaspoon grated orange peel
¼ cup cold water	

To blend cranberries: Put one ounce of orange juice into the blender. Blend the cranberries in the juice just until they have the consistency of a chopped food. Transfer to a bowl

124

and mash with a fork. Set aside. Soften the gelatine in the cold water, add the hot water and stir to dissolve thoroughly. Add the blended cranberries, sweetener, grated orange peel and the rest of the orange juice, and mix. Pour into ½ cup molds and chill. This is delicious on crisp lettuce.

Each cup is a fruit for the day.

AMERICAN   MARINATED ASPARAGUS

½ **cup tomato juice**	2 **tablespoons lemon juice**
1 **small clove garlic, diced**	1 **pound can asparagus,**
¼ **teaspoon salt**	**drained***
¼ **teaspoon dehydrated dill**	½ **cucumber, diced**
Dash black pepper	

Mix the first six ingredients in a bowl. Pour mixture over asparagus spears and top with the diced cucumber. Chill 3 hours.

*Refrigerate the liquid and drink it as an iced asparagus cocktail. I love this, and it has all the vitamins in it!

This recipe equals half a cup of tomato juice.

AMERICAN   APPLE-FILLED SQUASH

1 **large acorn or butternut**	1 **teaspoon ground**
squash, halved and	**cinnamon**
seeded	**About 2 capfuls No-**
4 **or 5 medium sized whole**	**Cal cherry syrup**
apples	

Cut 1 large acorn or butternut squash into 4 ounce wedges. On each wedge place one apple and sprinkle it with cinnamon and cherry syrup. Wrap each wedge in foil, sealing well. Bake in potato baker on top of stove or in 350° oven over a sheet of foil, 30 to 35 minutes (until squash is soft to pinch test). Serve in its foil coat.

Butternut squash tastes like sweet potato and apples. The acorn squash version will remind you of chestnuts and apples.

Each wedge equals a dinner vegetable and one fruit for the day.

AMERICAN   PICKLED BEETS AND ONIONS

1 **teaspoon pickling spices**	**Sliced beets**
⅓ **cup vinegar**	**Sliced onions**
Liquid non-sugar	
sweetener, 2 teaspoons	
or to taste	

Bring to boil the pickling spices, vinegar and sweetener. Pour marinade over the beets and onions and let stand over night.

Four ounces equals one dinner vegetable.

AMERICAN   UNLIMITED PICKLED
                      VEGETABLES

1 teaspoon pickling spices	3 or 4 red peppers,
1/3 cup vinegar	washed, seeded and
Liquid non-sugar sweet-	sliced
ener, 2 teaspoons or to	
taste	

Bring to boil the pickling spices, vinegar and non-sugar sweetener. Strain and pour over the peppers. Marinate overnight. Serve all you want as a side dish with all meats.

Also, try these unlimited pickled vegetables, using the same method and pickling marinade: drained bean sprouts, broccoli (fresh or frozen, raw or cooked), cauliflowerettes (fresh or frozen, raw or cooked), cucumbers, French-style string beans (frozen or canned), mushrooms, shredded cabbage.

AMERICAN   DW ZINGY KETCHUP

2 tablespoons horseradish	1 or 2 drops imitation
2 tablespoons tomato	butter flavoring
juice	1/4 teaspoon prepared
1 teaspoon lemon juice	mustard (optional for
2 or 3 drops liquid non-	more zingy flavor)
sugar sweetener	

Combine all and adjust to your taste. Can be stored 1 week in refrigerator.

AMERICAN   ZIPPY SALAD
                   DRESSING

1/2 teaspoon lemon Pills-	3 shakes of garlic powder
bury Funny Face	Small pinch oregano
powder	Small pinch thyme
1/2 teaspoon unflavored	Dash salt
gelatine	1/4 teaspoon white horse-
2 ounces water	radish
4 ounces tomato juice	
2 ounces white vinegar	

Combine the first three ingredients and let stand. In a small pan, heat the tomato juice, vinegar, garlic powder,

126

oregano, thyme leaves, salt and horseradish. As this starts to boil, add the gelatine mixture. Stir and let come to boil again. Immediately remove, cool and refrigerate. This is great over any salad or served cold over a hot vegetable you don't usually like. It adds an unusual flavor. Experiment by trying it over various vegetables.

The recipe equals four ounces of tomato juice.

GUESSING GAMES

GUESSING GAMES

In our groups we often have guessing sessions. I announce, "Today I'm going to give you a recipe for *mayonnaise!*" A roar comes back.

"EEK! What are you making it of *now?*"

"Guess!" I urge, and usually they can't. The answer is —mayonnaise from cauliflower! Here is how:

DW MAYONNAISE SPREAD
(Unlimited)

1 box frozen cauliflower, or 1 fresh cauliflower

2 tablespoons white vinegar

1 teaspoon liquid non-sugar sweetener

Salt to taste

Cook cauliflower according to directions on the box and then overcook. Drain well to remove all liquid. Put it through the blender with the vinegar and sweetener. Use with any vegetables you like—it's unlimited! Experiment with this spread: Season it further with sweetener or with salt (or other spice) to your taste.

Here's another Guessing Game dish—a rice that's unlimited! I use it in various dishes, but always add a sauce to give it special flavor. You'll find many of the sauces in the dishes that call for DW rice. Here's the simple basic recipe:

DW RICE
(Unlimited)

1 can bean sprouts, drained

Drain the bean sprouts and wash well in a collander under cold running water. Drain off all water. In chopping bowl, chop to a coarse consistency to look like rice. Add flavor according to main dish recipe.

128

One day I told a group, "Today I will give you a recipe for *candy*." Everyone looked at me with disbelief. A few moaned, others groaned. I began to give instructions for the recipe below. When I got to the statement, "Boil the grapefruit skin," a man's voice from the back of the room went, "*Oink! oink!*"

But this luscious candy won't make anyone look like a pig. Try it:

SWEET GRAPEFRUIT CANDY
(Unlimited)

½ **grapefruit**
1 **cup water**
¼ **cup No-Cal syrup,**
   any flavor
   Dash of nutmeg

Peel skin from one-half grapefruit and cut it into strips ½ inch wide. Boil the strips in the water until soft (about 10 minutes). Drain water. Add the No-Cal syrup and a dash of nutmeg to the pot and simmer until tender. Let cool, then remove the grapefruit candy from the cooking juice. Enjoy this sweet all you want. Try various No-Cal flavors—orange, cherry, grape, sour lemon or sour cherry.

The grapefruit segments, if you eat them, equal one fruit. The candy is unlimited.

Green Island Dressing is for luxuriating in Hawaii or some other South Sea Paradise. What's it made of? Look below:

GREEN ISLAND DRESSING

1 **can spinach, drained**   **Salt and pepper to**
½ **cup buttermilk**   **taste**

Put spinach and buttermilk through blender. Chill. Serve over a salad of sliced cucumber, green pepper, radishes and lettuce. Toss lightly. It's a delicacy!

This recipe equals half a cup of milk.

129

PARTIES ARE FOR SLIMMING!

NEVER TELL!

Never tell a guest you are serving diet food. Let people enjoy eating in your house just because the food is delicious.

At a recent New Year's Eve party in my home, I had invited a mix of people—some from my DW groups, and some personal friends. One couple were friends I have known for many years and included a husband who is a difficult guest because he is a truly picky eater. He drives his wife crazy because he won't eat this and he won't eat that.

I had prepared sweet-and-sour Swedish meat balls and the moment he saw me, he asked, "What are you serving?"

"I have thirty people to worry about," I said, "If you like the way it looks, eat it. If not, don't!"

"You're fresh!" he accused.

But during the evening I watched him. He went to the buffet and dug in for the Swedish meat balls—and he came back for more and more.

Since I had invited diet watchers that evening, I had no intention of making them break their diets. I had set out both non-diet foods (cake, liquor, champagne, dips and candy) and DW treats (limes and club soda—it makes a delicious drink, tomato juice, No-Cal syrups).

Out of the corner of my eye I watched my dieters, and they all watched me—and stayed on the diet. At midnight they put club soda and No-Cal syrup into champagne glasses, even the three girls in my group who were, I knew, the biggest cheats I had.

But I also watched my picky personal friend, who kept digging into the Swedish sweet-and-sour meatballs. At the end of the party as he was leaving, he asked if I had any left over. He wanted to take it home. Then I told him: "It's Diet Watchers Sweet-And-Sour Swedish meat balls!"

He said, calmly, "But my wife never makes meat balls so good!"

130

My picky guest didn't care whether it was diet food or not. He just wanted it to taste good. And he wanted something "new." Here is the recipe for the dish he loved:

SWEET AND SOUR SWEDISH MEAT BALLS
(Serves twelve)

2 **heads cabbage,** shredded	**Pinch black pepper**
16 **ounces tomato juice**	1 **glass water**
1 **tablespoon liquid non-** sugar sweetener	**Dash salt (optional)**
2 **tablespoons lemon juice**	12 **apples, green and tart**
4 **pounds chuck beef,** ground	

Shred the cabbage and put it on the bottom of a large pot. Add the tomato juice, liquid sweetener, lemon juice, and bring to a boil. Cover and reduce flame to a simmer. Taste and add lemon or sweetener for the sweet-and-sour flavor you prefer, then set aside. To the ground beef, add the black pepper and water, mixing thoroughly, and salt, if you like. Moisten your hands with cold water. With a teaspoon, pick up heaping spoonfuls of the beef mixture and roll them into tiny (1-inch) balls. Drop each gently into the simmering sauce and simmer 1 hour, covered. Then add the washed apples (do not peel, core or de-stem) and cook another half hour. Refrigerate. Skim off fat. Reheat to serve. Make this ahead and freeze it for a party. Freeze the apples in a separate plastic container with some sauce.

To serve this, I place the meat balls on a large bed of cabbage with a little sauce and I offer the rest of the hot sauce in a silver cream pitcher on the side, so guests can pour it over their own serving. I place the apples (hot or cold) on a side dish, to be taken as a garnish.

Six ounces of cooked beef equals one dinner portion. One apple is a fruit for the day.

COOK AHEAD FOR PARTIES

When you invite a crowd for dinner, cook and freeze ahead as much as possible, using the DW recipes you like best and do well. Just about every DW food can be frozen. To freeze meats, I use plastic containers with a good snap-on top. I fill them with food and liquid, and press out the air before sealing.

To press out air: I close the container, then lift one corner of the lid and use my thumb to press down hard on the center

131

of the cover. I can feel the air go out. Then I close the lid tightly all around again.

Always label the container for content and number of servings in it. When you need it, you'll have all the information you want right on the container, and the liquid for reheating right in it.

Use every other trick you know to cut down on party day oven cleaning and pot washing. For example, DW Party Stuffed Peppers are another wonderful recipe I use for freezable, free-me-the-hostess food. I can prepare it days (sometimes even weeks) ahead. And on the day of the party I can heat it on top of the stove. Top-of-stove heating when you entertain a large group of people is a great help—fast, convenient and no oven to clean!

PARTY STUFFED PEPPERS

(Serves 12)

24 large peppers (12 green, 12 red)	Pinch black pepper
	Dash salt
16-ounce can tomato juice	½ teaspoon parsley
	1 cup water
Lemon juice	4 cans bean sprouts
Liquid non-sugar sweetener	2 large cans mushrooms
	Sprigs of parsley
6 pounds ground beef	

In a large saucepan, combine the tomato juice, lemon juice and sweetener (two parts lemon juice to one part sweetener) and bring to a boil. Taste and add lemon juice or sweetener to get the winey flavor you prefer, and set aside. To the beef add black pepper, salt, parsley and water and mix thoroughly. Wash the peppers and cut off the tops. Scoop out the insides being careful not to crack or cut the peppers. Stuff the beef mixture into the peppers. Place them in a large deep baking pan, meat side up and touching so they hold each other up. Now pour the sweet and sour sauce over them. Bake 1 ½ hours in 350° oven. Refrigerate to chill and skim off fat. Freeze to store and reheat to serve.

When you serve: Heat the bean sprouts and mushrooms in separate pots. Drain them well. In large oval platter, make a bed of the drained sprouts. Top them with the mushrooms. Now make twelve indentations to hold the stuffed peppers. Arrange the red ones in the center and surround them with the green. Pour the sweet-and-sour sauce over all and garnish with sprigs of parsley.

Two stuffed peppers equal one dinner beef serving.

You can take the least expensive meats and most common foods and make them into delicious dishes—DW style —for a party. The recipes in the rest of this book include many of such low cost dishes—I believe in them. You can make them fun to eat.

Use colorful dishes, cloths, a centerpiece of flowers or other naturally colorful things (fresh vegetables, or orange gourds in the fall, for example) to make them festive.

Lighting is important. It helps you to show off the colors of foods. Remember that bright lights drain color out of foods. Try pink lights instead. For a party, I always remove the regular white lights of my dining table chandelier and put in pink ones. They are never noticed, but you'd be surprised at what they do for the food! Festive candles do the same.

MEATS NEED NOT BE HIGH COST

Inexpensive, slimming, delicious and easy to make are Sweet-and-Tangy Veal Balls. Serve them in a copper chafing dish that you keep hot over a candle warmer or on an electrically heated tray. Place a silver candlestick nearby and serve the sauce in a pretty pitcher.

SWEET AND TANGY VEAL BALLS

2 heads cabbage, shredded	Pinch black pepper
16 ounces tomato juice	1 glass water
1 tablespoon liquid non-sugar sweetener	Dash salt (optional)
2 tablespoons lemon juice	12 apples, green and tart
4 pounds lean veal, ground	

Shred the cabbage and line the bottom of a large pot with it. Add the tomato juice, liquid sweetener, lemon juice and bring to a boil. Taste for the sweet-and-sour flavor you prefer. Cover and reduce flame to a simmer. Now mix thoroughly the veal, pepper, water and salt and moisten your hands with cold water. With a teaspoon, pick up heaping spoonfuls of the veal mixture and roll into tiny balls. Gently drop each ball into the simmering sauce. Simmer 1 hour covered, then add the apples that have been washed but not peeled, cored or de-stemmed. Cook another half hour. Refrigerate. Skim off fat and reheat to serve.

I serve this in an oval party bowl, and spoon the meat balls onto a bed of the cabbage. I keep it hot over a candle warmer. I serve the sauce hot in a cream pitcher on the side, and guests pour it as they like over the balls. I reheat the apples and serve them on the side in a round platter.

Six ounces of veal balls equal one dinner portion. One apple is a fruit of the day.

CHICKENS "FOR MY FREEZER"

I always cook chickens "for my freezer" and never make less than four chickens at one time. I use one for an early meal and freeze three quickly in aluminum foil to serve as I need them. The freezer saves my cooking time.

It also saves money. I can buy foods when they are plentiful and low cost and enjoy them when they are expensive in the stores. It costs me no more to cook four chickens at once than it costs a neighbor of mine to buy a single rotisseried chicken at a not-so-fancy store in our area on Sundays.

And this habit always keeps me prepared for unexpected guests. I can offer them a party roast chicken half an hour after they have rung my bell.

HOW TO ROAST CHICKENS FOR FREEZING

3-pound broilers (whole)	**Small saucepan**
Paprika	**of additional water**
Garlic powder	**Paper toweling**
Parsley	**Aluminum foil**
6 **ounces water**	**Plastic container**

Clean the broilers and sprinkle them with paprika, garlic powder and parsley. Preheat oven to 350°. Place broilers breast side up (do not skin them) in a large uncovered roasting pan, adding 6 ounces of water. Set oven time for 1 hour and when it rings, turn the chickens breast side down. Reduce oven to 325° and set timer for ½ hour. When it rings, immediately remove roasting pan from oven. I always roast chickens on the second rack of my oven and on the bottom rack I place a small saucepan of water, keeping it filled throughout the cooking period. This keeps the oven moist so that the chickens brown without burning or drying. As soon as you remove chickens from oven, place them on large platter lined with 2 or 3 layers of paper toweling, to absorb fat drippings. Let cool 10 minutes only, then freeze each chicken separately.

TO FREEZE: I use 2 large (26-inch) sheets of aluminum foil, arranging them to overlap from three to six inches so that I have a large rectangle. I place each roasted chicken in the middle of the rectangle, wrap carefully to make an airtight package and freeze immediately.

I also save the roasting pan liquid drippings in a plastic container for DW gravy (see index). I refrigerate it, skim off the fat and then store it. This keeps one week in the refrigerator, or much longer in your freezer.

You can use these frozen chickens to make Southern Fry, a Broiled Chicken Platter, or Party Roast Chicken.

Southern Fried Chicken is an all-American favorite for parties because you can serve large groups of people easily in an informal, gay style:

SOUTHERN FRIED CHICKEN

Whole roasted chickens   ⅓ **cup dry powdered**
Roasting pan chicken   **skim milk**
dripping (½ cup)

The day before the party, defrost the chickens and cut them into single portion pieces as for southern fried chicken. Set aside. Place pan dripping (skim off any fat) in mixing bowl. Place dry milk powder in another bowl. Dip each piece of chicken into the liquid dripping and then into powder. Broil close to flame until brown.

Half a chicken equals one eating portion plus half a glass of milk for the day.

When I've served this to a large crowd everybody thinks I've been in the kitchen all day, but all I've done after 11 a.m. was go to have my hair done!

You can also make a broiled chicken platter from frozen roast chicken:

BROILED CHICKEN PLATTER

Defrost chickens the night before in your refrigerator. Cut as for southern fry and broil close to the flame to crisp (you can do this while the party is underway). I line my broiler rack with foil and avoid clean-up chores.

Half a chicken equals one eating portion for the day.

PARTY ROAST CHICKEN

Simply remove a whole chicken from the freezer, set oven at 500° and, leaving the chicken sealed in its foil wrap, bake it ½ hour on the second rack. It defrosts and heats to just the right doneness.

Here's another traditional American feast—turkey!—you can make ahead and that's always delicious cooked DW style:

STUFFED PARTY TURKEY

Large turkey (10 pounds or more)	16 ounces water
Paprika	Pan filled with water
Garlic Powder	Paper toweling
Parsley	Aluminum foil

Clean the turkey and sprinkle it with paprika, garlic powder and parsley, rubbing well inside and outside. Place turkey breast side up in a large roasting pan. Add 16 ounces of water. Put a pan filled with water on bottom rack of the oven and keep this filled. Place turkey on the rack above it in preheated 350° oven and roast 1 ½ hours. Turn turkey breast side down, lower flame to 325° and roast 1 hour longer. Turn again to put breast side up and test drumstick. When it moves easily, turkey is done. If not, continue roasting.

When done, remove from liquid immediately and place on a platter lined with several layers of paper toweling to absorb drippings. Let cool 10 minutes, then wrap in large sheets of foil to seal well. Freeze immediately. Pour drippings into jar and refrigerate. Skim fat from top and freeze in plastic container labeled as turkey liquid.

Day before the party: Transfer turkey and liquid from freezer to refrigerator. Do not reheat.

Day of the party: Remove turkey from refrigerator 4 hours before party. Carve and serve on party platters.

Six ounces of white meat equals one meat serving. Six ounces of dark meat equal one beef serving of the week.

A FREEZABLE STUFFING

I even make the stuffing ahead of time in a separate baking dish and I freeze it until the day of the party. I heat it on top of the stove or in the oven:

PARTY TURKEY GIBLET STUFFING

1 pound chicken or turkey giblets (don't use liver)	2 packages cauliflower, or 1 large head
2 stalks celery, diced fine	2 large cans mushrooms
1 chicken bouillon cube dissolved in 1 cup hot water	1 tablespoon soy sauce

Over a medium flame cook giblets and celery in the chicken bouillon about 1 hour, until giblets are tender. Cool and dice giblets into small pieces. Cook, drain and mash the cauliflower. Drain and dice the mushrooms. Now mix all ingredients well, including the soy sauce. Place in a large Corning ware baking dish and bake in 350° oven until top is brown (15 to 20 minutes). Freeze immediately.

Day before the party: Transfer from freezer to refrigerator.

Heat in 350° oven for 10 to 15 minutes just before serving.

One portion of stuffing equals one ounce of a turkey serving of white meat.

GRAVY FOR TURKEY AND STUFFING
(Unlimited)

Frozen turkey liquid with fat skimmed off

1 large can mushrooms, drained

Thaw frozen turkey liquid. Put through blender with drained mushrooms. When ready to serve, heat to boiling and transfer to pitcher.

CARVING AND SERVING PARTY TURKEY

Learn how to carve and serve foods gracefully. You are less likely to fall back on the old fattening foods when you are confident in presenting the slimming ones attractively.

Cooked turkey, defrosted or cold
Sharp carving knife
Serving platters
Paper lace doilies

Sprigs of parsley
Radish roses
Saran wrap
Gravy pitcher

To carve a turkey:

1. Remove drumsticks and separate them from the thighs.
2. Remove wings.
3. Break wings in half.
4. Arrange wings and drumsticks on one platter. Do not remove skin.
5. Arrange turkey breast side up.
6. Carve half the breast at a time. Begin to slice by starting at an angle and cutting toward the breast bone. Make very thin slices and leave a rim of skin around each slice.
7. Carve second half of breast.
8. Place paper lace doilies on platter and arrange turkey slices on it, starting on outside of platter and working toward the center. At the end, place a slice of turkey exactly in cen-

ter on top of the pyramid. Plan to set out two platters of white meat and top each with a cross of turkey wings. Arrange sprigs of parsley around the platter.

9. To carve the dark meat: Start slicing the turkey at bottom, working from the outside toward the breastbone. Again, slice very thin (the secret of avoiding a "dry" turkey taste).

10. Arrange on an oval platter, on lace paper doilies and again, starting at the outside, build a pyramid as you go to the center. Top with two drumsticks, arranged lengthwise with the thick parts touching in the middle of the platter. Set a radish rose where the two drumsticks meet. Garnish with parsley sprigs.

11. Cover everything tightly with Saran wrap and let stand at room temperature until serving time.

RADISH ROSES

Small red radishes   **Cold water**
Jar

Wash radishes well and cut off the tops and bottoms. Make 4 vertical cuts from the top to half way down each radish. Fill jar with cold water and drop in the radishes. Crisp in refrigerator ½ hour to make flower petals open. Remove immediately from water and use as radish garnishes.

DW ONE POT PARTY COOKING

My one pot DW cooking was, as I admit, a holdover from when I was fat. When I began to experiment with the DW foods, wanting to keep my one pot cooking, I devised a few tricks so that I could use one large pot for several ingredients of a meal.

When I cook for crowds, I cut down on pot-washing by using a really large pot and making inside "cups" of heavy gauge aluminum in which I cook four vegetables at once. The aluminum cups are easy to bend into shape, and hold their position. I can fit four cups into my 12-quart pot.

I fill each cup with a vegetable, just covering it with water, (I don't go to the top of the cup or the water will overflow). When done, I lift each cup with a pair of tongs. The kind you use when you sterilize baby bottles are perfect for this, but any kind will do. Or to avoid burns I use protective kitchen mittens so I can grasp the aluminum cups firmly.

Not only have I gotten four vegetables cooked in one pot, and used only one burner, I don't have to work hard to wash my pot. No food has touched it, since the vegetables have cooked in the aluminum liners. The less work for me, the more I can enjoy my own parties!

HOW TO MAKE DW GELS

Some early copies of the Diet Watchers Guide did not have a recipe for DW Gel, which we included in menu plans. We received so many hundreds of requests for the recipe that we added it to later editions. But in case your copy happens to lack it, here are two ways to make it:

DW GEL # 1

2 envelopes gelatine, unflavored	2 envelopes Pillsbury Funny Face, any flavor you like
	8 cups of water

Dissolve gelatine in four cups of water. Heat, adding Funny Face and stirring until it boils. Shut flame. Add 4 cups of cold water and stir well. Pour into sherbet glasses for individual servings and chill to set. Buy enough Funny Face during the summer months, when the stores are well stocked, to last you through the winter and you can enjoy this all year around. Unlimited!

If you failed to stock up on Funny Face or can't find it where you live, here is another way to make it:

DW GEL # 2

1 bottle diet soda, any flavor you like	1 envelope unflavored gelatine

Remove cap from bottle of diet soda and let stand until all bubbles escape (about 15 to 20 minutes). Dissolve gelatine in two cups of cold soda. Heat 2 cups of remaining soda and combine, stirring well. Pour into sherbet glasses and chill in refrigerator to set. Good! Unlimited!

MAKE YOUR OWN SYRUPS

If you have trouble finding a commercial brand, there are easy ways to make tasty Diet Watchers syrups and use them in recipes just as you would use the brands in the DW recipe ingredients lists. Try these:

DW SYRUP # 1

1 tablespoon Pillsbury Funny Face powder, any flavor	¼ cup water

Combine. Add Funny Face powder, to adjust for the sweetness you like. Since this is sold mainly as a summer drink, stock up in summer with a big supply to take you through the winter months.

Here is another way to make your own syrup:

DW SYRUP # 2

1 tablespoon liquid non-sugar sweetener	**2 or 3 drops of vegetable coloring**
¼ cup water	**Dash cinnamon (optional)**

Combine the first three ingredients and adjust for sweetness, adding sweetener if you prefer. And try adding that dash of cinnamon—you'll like it!

A WORD ABOUT SUBSTITUTIONS

Many people have written to us that where they live they cannot find a specific product that we name in a DW recipe. I suggest certain brand names because they are easily available to me. Most of them are national brands. But if they are not available where you live, look for similar products. For example, I mention Coleman's English mustard. You may find a similar product in a local store known simply as "*powdered* mustard."

Another example has been the non-calorie flavored syrups. If your local store does not carry the brand I name, ask the store manager to stock it. Also, I use La Choy brand bean sprouts because I find their crunchy texture tastes better in my recipes. I recommend Kikkoman soy sauce to all my diet watchers because of its taste and because it has no sugar.

Or you can write to the company that manufacturers the brand and ask how you can get it. Here are the addresses of companies whose brands are used in DW recipes:

La Choy Bean Sprouts:
Division of
Beatrice Foods Co.
Archbold, Ohio
43502

Kikkoman soy sauce:
Kikkoman International, Inc.
11-31 31st Avenue
Long Island City
New York 11102

No-Cal syrups:
No-Cal Corporation
919 Flushing Avenue
Brooklyn, New York 11206

Pillsbury Funny Face powders:
Pillsbury Company
608 Second Avenue, South
Minneapolis, Minnesota
55402

MENU PLANS FOR TWO WEEKS AROUND THE WORLD

Have you ever looked up at a jet airliner streaking across the sky and wished you were up there inside, adventuring around the world? You can make an eating-travel adventure with the Diet Watchers recipes. Have the best eating of every country—the new tastes and combinations (but not the faults!). If you don't want to "travel" for two weeks, even in your imagination, you can take a week or just a "day" off, exploring the foods of any country on this trip, any day of the week, and becoming slim as you "go" . . .

SUNDAY IN FRANCE

First Day

8 a.m. BREAKFAST
* ½ grapefruit
  Two croissants
  Coffee with milk

LUNCH
Consomme with croutons
Shrimp casserole Francaise
*Sliced fresh pear
Coffee

AFTERNOON SNACK
One glass of milk stirred with 2 capfuls No-Cal
    strawberry syrup—on the rocks

DINNER
Broccoli soup
Braised chicken livers
Spinach
Tossed green salad
* ½ cantaloupe
Coffee with milk

141

EVENING SNACK
French fried cauliflowerettes
One glass diet soda

*Three fruits of the day

MONDAY HOPOVER TO ENGLAND

Second Day

8 a.m. BREAKFAST

Tomato juice, 4 ounces
Soft-boiled egg in a cup
Cinnamon toast with orange marmalade*

LUNCH

Orange juice, 4 ounces*
Mustard broiled mackeral, 4 ounces
Tossed green salad
1 slice toast
Tea with milk

AFTERNOON SNACK

Tea with milk
Grapefruit candy

DINNER

Watercress soup
Kidney pie
Lettuce salad
*2-inch wedge of honeydew melon
Coffee

EVENING SNACK

DW Gel
Tea with milk

*Three fruits of the day

TUESDAY SKOL IN SCANDINAVIA

Third Day

8 a.m. BREAKFAST
Tomato juice, 4 ounces
Swedish steamed egg
Coffee with milk

LUNCH
Spicy cooked shrimp
1 slice toast
Green salad
DW Gel
Coffee with milk

AFTERNOON SNACK
* ½ cup strawberries
Coffee with milk

DINNER
Smorgasbord table (choose six ounces of seafood)
Marinated celery chunks
Cucumber-onion salad, 2 ounces
Beet and onion salad, 2 ounces
* ½ cantaloupe in bowl, mixed with sections of
one orange
Coffee with milk

EVENING SNACK

Finish milk for the day

*Three fruits of the day

WEDNESDAY RUSSIAN HOLIDAY

Fourth day

8 a.m. CONTINENTAL BREAKFAST

Orange juice, 4 ounces*
Hard boiled egg with salt
1 slice toast
Coffee with 2 ounces of milk

LUNCH
Mock borscht
Poached fish with mushroom stuffing
Salad of greens
Toast
Tea with lemon

AFTERNOON SNACK

1 glass schav (mix in 2 ounces of buttermilk
as "smetana")

DINNER

* ½ grapefruit
Beef stroganoff
DW rice
Green salad
Tea with lemon

BEDTIME SNACK

* ½ cup strawberries in bowl with 4 ounces buttermilk
"smetana" topping, sweetened to taste with non-
sugar sweetener if you like or use 2 capfuls straw-
berry No-Cal syrup. Finish milk for the day

THURSDAY IN SUNNY ITALY

Fifth Day

8 a.m. BREAKFAST
*Honey dew melon, 2-inch slice
Asparagi-cheese breakfast
Coffee with milk

LUNCH
Scallops scampi
Hot garlic bread (one slice)
Black coffee or espresso
Escarole salad

AFTERNOON SNACK

Dish DW spaghetti
Glass of skim milk

DINNER

Antipasto
Chicken oregano
Garlic vegetable dish
Fried Italian peppers
Sautéed fagiolini
Lemon fennel
*Fresh orange segments
Black coffee or espresso

EVENING SNACK

* ½ cantaloupe
Finish milk for the day

*Three fruits of the day

FRIDAY—START LONG WEEKEND
OF SHORT FLYING SIDE TRIPS

Sixth Day

9 a.m. BREAKFAST IN RUMANIA

*Orange juice, 4 ounces
Rumanian latkis
Coffee with milk

LUNCH IN GREECE

Lemoned cod
Large tossed green salad
1 slice bread toasted
Coffee with milk

AFTERNOON SNACK

Tall glass of tomato juice

DINNER IN GREECE

Greek beefsteaks
Large serving DW rice
Greek salad
Side dish of sliced tomato, 2 ounces
Greek mushrooms
*Fresh pear
Coffee with milk

EVENING SNACK—JUST LANDED IN GERMANY

*Apple and sauerkraut snack

BEDTIME SNACK

One glass of milk
DW Gel

*Three fruits of the day

SATURDAY WANDERING

Seventh Day

8 a.m. BREAKFAST

*Orange juice, 4 ounces
Bavarian egg-in-a-frame with round toast
Coffee (black)

LUNCH IN GERMANY

Tomato juice, 4 ounces
Sweet-and-sour fish
Tossed green salad
1 slice of bread
Coffee (black)

AFTERNOON SNACK

Coffee
DW Orange Gel

DINNER (HUNGRY IN HUNGARY?)

* ½ grapefruit
  Chicken paprikash
  Sweet-and-sour cabbage
  Coffee (black)

NIGHTTIME SNACK

  Glass of buttermilk
*Sliced apples topped with a dash of cinnamon and
  2 capfuls of No-Cal syrup

*Three fruits of the day

SUNDAY FLIGHT TO THE ORIENT

Eighth Day

9 a.m. BREAKFAST ON PLANE

* ½ grapefruit
  Poached egg
  1 slice toast
  Coffee with milk

LUNCH IN INDIA

  Tuna curry
  Madras cucumber chutney
  DW rice
*Major Lee's pineapple chutney
  1 slice toast
  Coffee with milk

AFTERNOON SNACK

  Iced black coffee
*Sliced apple in bowl of skim milk

DINNER IN IRAN

  Eastern stuffed eggplant
  Black coffee
  Tossed green salad

147

EVENING SNACK

8 ounce glass tomato juice

*Three fruits of the day

MONDAY FAR EASTERN EXOTICISMS
Ninth Day

9 a.m. BREAKFAST ON WINGS

Tomato juice, 4 ounces
Soft-boiled egg
Cinnamon toast
Coffee with milk

LUNCH ON LAND (JAPAN)

* ½ grapefruit
Japanese lemon fish
DW rice
Tossed green salad with vinegared cucumber slices
1 slice bread
Tea

AFTERNOON SNACK (HAWAII)

*Tangy fruit cocktail

DINNER

Hawaiian Island chicken
Cucumber salad with Green Island dressing
DW rice
*Island relish
Coffee with milk

EVENING SNACK

Finish milk for the day

*Three fruits of the day

CANADIAN TUESDAY
(HEADING HOME VIA THE NORTHERN ROUTE)

Tenth Day

9 a.m. BREAKFAST

Tomato juice, 4 ounces
*Cherry-pear pancakes
Coffee with milk

MIDMORNING SNACK

Coffee with milk

LUNCH

Tuna pie casserole
Tossed green salad
Tea with lemon

AFTERNOON SNACK

Dish of cherry DW Gel
Coffee with milk

DINNER

Salmon croquettes
Spinach salad
French fried cauliflowerettes
* ½ cup blueberries
Coffee with milk

EVENING SNACK

*Molded apple cider salad
Finish milk for the day

*Three fruits of the day

WEDNESDAY—BACK IN THE GOOD OLD USA
(West Coast)

Eleventh Day

8 a.m. BREAKFAST

  *Orange juice, 4 ounces
   Cottage cheese griddle cakes
   Coffee with milk

  LUNCH

  Creamed mushroom soup
  *Stuffed grapefruit
   Coffee with milk
   Toast

  AFTERNOON SNACK

  Tomato juice, 4 ounces

  DINNER

  Stuffed breast of veal
  Green salad with four ounces combined sliced
    tomato and onion
  Coffee with milk
  *DW Gel

  EVENING SNACK

  Finish milk for the day
  * ½ cantaloupe

  *Three fruits of the day

THURSDAY SOUTHERN DRAWLS

Twelfth Day

BREAKFAST

  Tomato juice, 4 ounces
  *George Washington pancakes
   Coffee with milk

LUNCH

Southern salmon bake
Marinated cucumber slices
Green salad
Coffee with milk

AFTERNOON SNACK

1 glass skim milk mixed with one capful cherry No-
  Cal syrup

DINNER

Tomato juice, 4 ounces
Roast "pork" dinner
Green salad with DW zingy ketchup
*Apple filled squash
*Honeydew melon 2-inch wedge
  Coffee with milk

EVENING SNACK

Orange DW Gel
Finish milk for the day

*Three fruits of the day

FRIDAY MIDWESTERN TWANG

Thirteenth Day

BREAKFAST

*Orange juice, 4 ounces
  Country breakfast
  Coffee with milk

LUNCH

Tomato juice, 4 ounces
Shrimp Creole
1 slice bread, toasted (or with DW mayonnaise
  spread)
* ½ small cantaloupe
  Coffee with milk

AFTERNOON SNACK

DW Gel
Glass of buttermilk

DINNER

*Frankfurter surprise dinner
 Salad of lettuce with four ounces tomato slices
 Zippy salad dressing
 Coffee with milk

EVENING SNACK

Finish milk for the day

*Three fruits of the day

SATURDAY SWINGING IN INTERNATIONAL
NEW YORK

Fourteenth Day

EYE-OPENER BREAKFAST

Tomato juice on rocks (1 ice cube) with wedge of
 lemon juice
Lemon mushrooms on toast with bull's-eye egg
Coffee with milk

LUNCH

* ½ grapefruit
 New England shrimp with mushrooms
 Large tossed green salad
 Coffee (black)

AFTERNOON SNACK

*Cranberry salad
 Coffee with milk

DINNER

Turkish kabobs
French fried onions
Large green salad with vinaigrette sauce
Braised Belgian endive
*Sliced pear in DW syrup
Black coffee

EVENING SNACK

Finish milk for the day

*Three fruits of the day

When I was fat, Sunday was *my* day, the best day of the week. Even when the children were small I'll loll in bed late. Once I was dressed I'd ask my husband, *"Where are we going today?"* Sunday we always went out to eat in a restaurant.

If you go out to restaurants on Sunday, look around. The first thing you notice is fat people. Restaurants are always filled with fat people on Sundays. They are having their weekly pleasure—eating their poisons.

Women in my groups ask me, "But what do you do on *Sunday*? What shall I do when we all go out to Sunday dinner?"

They want to diet all during the week, and go out to eat in order to have a "good time" on Sunday.

Sunday is their day for self-pity. After all, you work hard all week: Sunday is "your day off." Sunday is a day you "owe to yourself."

They think they'll escape their fat bodies on Sunday. Actually, they are using Sunday to destroy themselves. Actually, they are planning *a day away* from themselves.

Let's agree, Sunday is a day for enjoyment, for relaxation. So why fight the crowds in restaurants?

Instead of eating out, why not cook *ahead*? Cook Sunday morning, or a day ahead, or a week or more ahead if you have a freezer. Plan a special *new* DW dish—or an old favorite. Get dinner ready in the morning, go out for fun— which means *activity* (bowl, walk, ice skate, take a drive, see a movie, visit a friend), and *come home to eat*.

What I especially resent about Sunday eating out is that the restaurants offer you so little variety in their menus that they tempt you to slide back to the old foods. The most common combination you'll find is meat, peas and potatoes (mashed or fried). But if you eat at home Sundays you can offer yourself the most tempting variety of the proper

Diet Watchers foods, the ones that keep slimming you down.

Now that I am slim I don't go out to eat on Sundays. I *like* to cook new dishes on weekends. I am not looking to escape my kitchen and my house. I am looking to enjoy it.

But when you do go out to eat, *don't eat the poisons*. Select from the menu. Have a proper, well balanced meal. You want a holiday? Fat doesn't take a holiday! Anytime you take a holiday from proper eating your fat, stays right with you.

DON'T CHEAT WORK SHEETS

If you begin sliding back to the old foods, you will begin lying to yourself again. *Lying to yourself* is what keeps you fat. The most important thing I do for my groups is to show people the ways in which they lie to themselves.

"I am like a mother who has five children," I sometimes tell a group. "But one of those five is a rotten child. What does this mother do? Whom does she protect? *The rotten one*!

"Why? Because she feels the hurts of the rotten one. She knows that's the one who will do things wrong. *All* rotten kids do things wrong, and get hurt. So that's the one she watches most closely, the one she tries to guide most carefully, the one that she knows needs most protection—in short, the rotten kid is the one she "loves" the most.

"You," I tell a DW group, "are like my rotten kid. I *know* you'll cheat. I have to watch you and catch your cheating. I have to *make* you admit it to yourself when you cheat."

You, reader, are going to cheat. But here are worksheets to help you catch any little lies to yourself, and truly reach your slimness goal.

MY SLIMNESS TARGET

PRESENT SCALE WEIGHT_____

MY GOAL_____   ╱

TARGET DATE_____

NUMBER OF WEEKS TO GOAL_____
    (Estimate)

PRESENT DRESS SIZE_____
    (Women)

PRESENT BELT SIZE_____

(Men)
TARGET SIZE_____
  (Dress or Belt)
DAILY EATING RECORD
(list amounts you eat)

BREAKFAST
  TIME_____
  JUICE_____
  BREAD_____
  PROTEIN_____
  BEVERAGE_____
  OTHER_____
  ANY CHEATING FOODS?_____

MIDMORNING SNACK_____
  HOUR_____
  ANY CHEATING?_____

LUNCH
  HOUR_____
  APPETIZER_____
  BREAD_____
  PROTEIN_____
  VEGETABLES_____
  DESSERT_____
  PORTION SIZES CORRECT?_____
  BEVERAGE_____
  ANY CHEATING?_____

MIDAFTERNOON SNACK_____
  HOUR_____
  CHEATING?_____

DINNER
  HOUR_____
  APPETIZER_____
  MAIN DISH_____

VEGETABLES_____

SIDE DISHES_____

SALAD_____

DESSERT AND DRINK_____

PORTION SIZES CORRECT?_____

ANY CHEATING?_____

EVENING SNACK_____

   HOUR_____

   GLASSES OF MILK DURING THE DAY_____

   TOMATO JUICE TAKEN TODAY_____

   BREAD EATEN TODAY_____

   FRUITS EATEN TODAY_____

WEEKLY CHART

START   (scale weight)_____

FAT LOSS (since last week)_____

DRESS OR BELT SIZE NOW_____

CHEATING TO OMIT THIS WEEK_____

OTHER CHANGES TO MAKE THIS WEEK_____

_____

_____

FAT LOSS GOAL FOR NEXT WEEK_____

NEW DW DISH TO COOK NEXT WEEK_____

_____

_____

SO BE A COOK!

(Pronounced *Kook*)

Eight years ago, when I first went on the DW diet, I was invited to a friend's dinner party. We were dieting together then, but I knew how badly she cheated. So I asked her what she was serving at her party. "Roast beef," she assured me. I asked her how she was making it.

She looked annoyed. "On the rotisserie," she said.

That was all right. But I also knew *all* the ways she cheated. I knew the size of portions she served. On the night of the party I brought my little postage scale with me. Right at the table, with five couples seated, I weighed out my slices of roast beef. They all roared with laughter at this *kook*!

Not long ago I got together with the same group. We recalled that incident and laughed about it.

Then I looked at them. They are *fat*. They wear sizes 16, 18 and 20. They looked at me. I wear a size nine.

I guess we were all thinking the same thing. My fat friends said to me, wistfully, "You know, you weren't such a kook . . ."

INDEX

Antipasto, 34
Apple(s)
 and cabbage chutney, 89
 and sauerkraut, 70
 -filled squash, 125
Artichokes, Near-Eastern, 91
Asparagus, marinated, 125
Aspic glace, 44

Bean sprout(s)
 fried (Chinese), 100
 garlic vegetable dish, 36
 orange, 102
 As substitute for noodles, rice and spaghetti:
 peppered "noodles" (Hungarian), 72
 DW "rice," 128
 salad (Chinese), 101-102
 DW style "spaghetti," 38
 and meat balls, 32
Beef
 balls (Hawaiian), 105
 boiled (Irish), 65
 braised, 41-42
 chile con carne, 113
 flanken (Jewish), 54-55
 with knoble-borscht, 56-57
 goulash supreme, 72
 hamburger steaks (Greek), 76
 kabobs, 89
 luau (Hawaiian), 104
 meatballs, sweet and sour, 131
 sauerbraten, 69
 steak
 pepper (Chinese), 97

Rumanian muschi, 74
 teriyaki, 95
 stroganoff, 82
 stuffed peppers, 132
 tenderloin, broiled Rumanian, 73-74
Beet(s)
 with apples, 67
 and onion salad, 80
 pickled, and onions, 125-126
Beverages
 Hawaiian fruit cocktail, 108
 unlimited, 17
Bouillabaisse, 41
Bread
 cinnamon toast, 62
 "croissant," 39
 croutons, 40
 diet rules for, 18
 garlic, hot, 27
Breakfast
 country (American), 115
 Sparagi cheese dish. 27
Broccoli soup, 48
Brussels sprouts, lemon, 68

Cabbage
 and mushrooms (Chinese), 100
 -apple chutney, 89-90
 cake, sweet and sour, 70
 curried, 90
 marinated Chinese, 107-108
 red, cucumber salad, 70
 sweet and sour (Hungarian), 73
Candy, grapefruit, 129
Carrots

and butternut tzimmes ("chulant"), 55, 59
 braised, 66
Casserole(s)
 Aegean, 75-76
 chicken, 43
 shrimp, Francaise, 46
 Tuna pie, 109
Cauliflower
 french fried, 111
 "pasta," 27-28
 mayonnaise spread, 128
 soup, 48
Celery
 braised, 49
 marinated, 79-80
Cheese
 breakfast, Sparagi, 27
Chicken
 a la King, 43
 and antipasto, 29
 arroz con pollo, 112-113
 boiled, and soup (Jewish), 55-56
 broiled, 135
 burgers, 106
 cacciatore, 29
 casserole, 43
 chow mein, 96
 -cucumber soup dinner, 93
 curried, 86
 dumplings (Jewish), 54
 fried
 Chinese, 96
 Southern, 135
 Hawaiian, 104
 oregano, 29

oriental, 85-86
paella, 114
paprikash, 71-72
roast
  for freezing, 134-135
  party, 135-136
romano, 30
with mushrooms, 30
Chicken livers
  braised, 42
  chopped (Jewish), 54
  en brochette, 42
Chile con carne
  beef, 113
  veal, 113
Chop suey, 99-100
Chow mein
  chicken, 96
  shrimp, 98
  subgum, 99
Chutney
  apple-cabbage, 89-90
  lemon, 90
  madras cucumber, 90
  pepper, 90
  pineapple, 91
Cranberry salad, 124
Cod
  See Fish
Cucumber(s)
  and red cabbage salad
    (German), 70
  boats, stuffed, remoulade, 47
  chutney, madras, 90
  drums, stuffed with meat, 65-66
  -onion salad, 79
Curry
  bake, shrimp, 86-87
  cabbage, 90
  chicken, 86
  lamb, 87-88
  scallop and shrimp, 88
  tuna, 85

Diet Watcher's system, 19-25

Eggplant
  leftover, Mid-Eastern
    surprise, 91
  marinated garlic, 37
  steak, 60
  stuffed with veal, 30-31
  vinete (Rumanian), 74
  with mushroom stuffing, 36
  zucchini surprise, 37
Egg(s)
  in a frame, 68
  griddle cakes, 115-116
  hard boiled, in spinach, 39
  Swedish, steamed, 77
Endive, braised, 67
Escarole
  boiled, 34
  salad, 34
  sautéed, 35

Fennel, lemon, 35
Fish
  American fry, 118
  baked Hawaiian, 103
  balls, smorgasbord, 78
  bouillabaisse, 41
  brook trout, barbecued, 119
  carp
    baked, 52-53
    boiled, 53-54
  cod
    lemon, grilled, 75
    stuffing, for cucumbers, 47
  diet rules for, 18
  fillets, baked, stuffed, 81
  finnan haddie, 64
  gefilte, 56
  mackerel

mustard broiled, 62-63
sweet and sour, 69-70
pike, with mushroom
  stuffing, 81
quenelles, 45
salmon
  bake, Southern, 117
  dumplings, 110
  Swedish sweet and sour, 77
Shad
  baked, 53
  roe, 122
sweet and sour, 68-69
swordfish
  lemon, 94
  smorgasbord, 79
tuna
  chowder, 110
  curry, 85
  pie, 109
  roe, 122
  stuffing, for grapefruit,
    117-118
Frankfurter(s)
  dinner, surprise, 120
  sausage goulash, 72
  skewered (Hawaiian), 103
Franks, "special"
  in stuffed peppers, 31
  remoulade, 45
  stuffed, kosher style, 57
Fruit cocktail, 108

Gazpacho, 71
Gels, DW, 139
Goulash
  sausage, 72
  supreme (Hungarian), 72
Grapefruit
  candy, sweet, 129
  stuffed with tuna, 117-118
Gravy, turkey, 137
Griddle cakes
  cottage cheese, 115
  Egg, 115-116
  See also Pancakes

Hors d'oeuvre and Appetizers
  antipasto, 34
  fruit cocktail, Hawaiian, 108
  mushroom, 50
  peppers, fried Italian, 35-36
  vegetable, 50

Kabobs
  Hawaiian, 103
  lamb (shish kabob), 88
  pineapple scallops, 121-122
  Turkish, 89
Ketchup, DW zingy, 126
Kidney pie, 63
Kugel, holiday, 59-60

Lamb
  Aegean casserole, 75
  and pineapple burgers, 106
  Armenian, 85
  breast of, barbecued, 118-119
  chops, savory (Hawaiian), 107
  curry, 87-88
  shish kabob, 88
  riblet surprise, (Japanese), 93
  ribs teriyaki (Japanese), 94
  roast, Hawaiian, 105
Latkis, Rumanian, 73
Lemon chutney, 90
Limited foods, 17-19
Liver(s)
  braised, chicken, 42
  chicken, en brochette, 42
  chopped chicken (Jewish), 54
  vegetarian, 52
Lobster

boats glace, 44
Chinese delight, 96-97
Delaware, 123
Florida, 120
mousse, 120-121
Lo-mein, lobster, 98

Mackerel
Marmalade, English orange, 62
Mayonnaise spread, 128
Meat, diet rules for, 18
Mushroom(s)
  and cabbage (Chinese), 100
  Chekhov style, 84
  garlic vegetable dish, 36
  Greek, 76
  hors d'oeuvre, 50
  Irish, braised, 66
  lemon, on toast, 116
  -pepper stuffing, for fish, 81
  smorgasbord bowl, 80
  soup
    creamed, 124
    Russian, 83
  -sprouts stuffing, for veal,
    57-58
  stuffing for eggplant, 36
  with herbs, Near-Eastern, 92
Mustard
  Chinese, hot, mild, 102

Nasi goreng (Dutch), 67
"Noodles"
  See Bean sprouts

Onion(s)
  and pickled beets, 125-126
  french fried, 49-50
  soup, French, 48
Orange(s)
  marmalade, English, 62
  sauce (Chinese), 102
  sprouts, 102
Oysters, royale, 63-64

Paella, 114
Pancakes
  cherry-pear (Canadian), 109
  George Washington, 116
  Rumanian latkis, 73
  See also Griddle cakes
Party foods, 130-140
Pasta(s), Italian, 27-28
  See also Bean sprouts
Pea(s)
  pods, Chinese, 101
  soup, 48-49
Pepper(s)
  boats, for shrimp, 46
  chutney, 90
  fried Italian style, 35-36
  roasted ("pepperoni"), 37-38
  steak (Chinese), 97
  stuffed, party, 132
  stuffed with sausage, 31
Pineapple
  chutney, Major Lee's, 91
  compote, stewed, 61
"Pork"
  See Veal,
Poultry, diet rules for, 18
  See also Chicken; Rock
    Cornish hen; Turkey

Quenelles, 45

Rabbit, roasted, 31
Radish roses, 136
Relish, Hawaiian, 107
"Rice," DW
  See Bean sprouts
Rock Cornish hen, barbecued, 119

Salad dressing(s)

dill, 61
garlic-vinegar (Italian), 36
green island (Hawaiian), 129
mayonnaise spread, DW, 128
sour-cream horseradish, 61
sweet and sour, 84
zippy, 126-27
Salad(s)
  beet and onion, 80
  cranberry, 124
  cucumber-onion, 79
  escarole, 34
  Greek, 76
  Jewish spring, 60-61
  molded apple cider, 111
  "rice" (Chinese), 101-102
  Roman, 38
  spinach, summer, 111
  tomato, stuffed, 108
Salmon
  See Fish
Sauces
  braised beef, DW, 42
  gravy, for turkey, 137
  ketchup, zingy, 126
  mustard, Chinese (hot and
    mild), 102
  orange (Chinese), 102
  remoulade, 46-47
  vinaigrette, 51
Sauerbraten, 69
Sauerkraut and apples, 70
Sausage, Italian,
  See Franks, "special" kosher
Scallops
  and pineapple kabobs, 121-122
  and shrimp curry, 88
  creamed, New England, 121
  scampi, 28
  tempura, 94
Schav
  See Sorrel leaves
Shad
  See Fish
Shellfish
  Paella, 114
  See also Lobster; Oysters;
    Scallops; Shrimp
Shish kabob, 88
Shrimp
  and scallop curry, 88
  bake, curry, 86-87
  butterfly (Chinese), 95-96
  casserole Francaise, 46
  chow mein, 98
  Creole, 123
  Delaware, 123

nasi goreng (Dutch), 67
pepper boats remoulade, 46
scampi, 32
spicy smorgasbord, 78
Sorrel leaves
  beverage (Russian), 83-84
  with sour cream, 60
Soups
  Armenian, green, 89
  Borscht
    knoble-, 58
    with flanken, 56-57
    mock, 83
    Old Russian, 83
    Russian, 82-83
  bouillabaisse, 51
  broccoli, 48
  cauliflower, cream of, 48
  chicken
    -cucumber (Japanese), 93
    Jewish, 55-56
  Chinese vegetable, 99
  consomme, with croutons, 40
  gazpacho, 71
  mushroom
    creamed, 124
    Russian, 83
  onion, French, 48
  pea
    green, 48-49
    split
      with croutons, 40
      with noodles (Jewish), 59
  tuna chowder, 110
  vegetable (Jewish), 58-59
  vichyssoise, 49
  watercress, 64
"Spaghetti"
  See Bean sprouts,
Spinach
  breakfast surprise, 39
  green island dressing, 129
  salad, 111
Squash
  butternut, and carrot tzimmes,
    55,59
  holiday kugel, 59-60
  stuffed with apple, 125
  sweet and sour, 32-33
  See also Zucchini
String beans
  Chinese, 101
  garlic vegetable dish, 36
  saute, 35
Stuffing, party, for freezing,
  136-137
Substitutions for ingredients, 140

Sweetbreads parisienne, 44
Swordfish
  See Fish
Syrups, DW, 139-140

Taboo foods, 19
Tempura, scallop, 94
Teriyaki
  lamb ribs, 94
  steak, 95
Tomatoes
  sour, 71
  stuffed, 108
Tuna
  See Fish
Turkey
  Hawaiian skewered, 103
  stuffed, party, 136
  to carve and serve, 137-138
Tzimmes, carrot and butternut,
  55, 59

Unlimited foods, 16-17

Veal
  and zucchini (Sicilian), 75
  balls, sweet and tangy, 133
  blanquette, 47
  breast of
    stuffed, Jewish style, 57
    stuffed, American style,
      123-124
  Caesar's, 28
  chile con carne, 113
  chops
    barbecued, 119
    with brown sauce, 124
  eggplant stuffed with, 30-31
  roast (American), 122
  as mandarin spare ribs, 95
  as "Roast Pork" substitute:
    Chinese, 97-98
    dinner, American, 122
Vegetable(s)
  hors d'oeuvre, 50
  limited, 17
  pickled, unlimited, 126
Venison
  roast, 33
  steaks, 33
Vichyssoise, 49

Watercress soup, 64

Zucchini
  and veal (Sicilian), 75
  surprise, with eggplant, 37